Falling Out of Love With My Career

KC Shomler

Bonfire Books Press

Contents

Dedication

For Steven Shomler, My life change champion.

I could have done this without you, but so happy I didn't have to!

Foreword

This manuscript came to me as I was bathing in my own cold, deep and enormous pool of uncertainty, without an obvious shore to pull out on. Like KC, a sudden death of a sibling on top of the rest of the pile of stacked disappointments woke me to the realization that I was in a painful transition and I was resisting. My ambition for the proverbial "right set" of life descriptors was resulting in more and more suffering. I, too, had fallen out of love with my professional life and could not find a way to accommodate my constant inner struggle within the tense environment of medical practice. My sister's death and my loss of her reflective support stole the last bit of perseverance I could muster.

KC's real-time, candid, messy and vulnerable expressions of her journey through change accompanied by real and confusing emotional angst help us know we are not alone and everyone has to face transition. Life truly is unpredictable and it hurts to make choices that involve others. Being a hopeful person by nature as well as a "fixer of problems", I found her words to provide solace for my self-judgment and seeming internalized failures. The book is raw, honest and timely.

I first read her manuscript before giving my notice at my current job, after I had awoken to the desire to step away from the practice of medicine. The book helped me re-evaluate my professional situation through a more open-hearted and self-compassionate lens. I was able to see a path forward completely apart from my identity as a doctor. Her shared experience helped me find a way to resign from medicine with hope for a new start. In the months after, as I have ended my tenure, I have re-read the book a few more times. It soothes me. It is a "thank you for the experience and the lessons learned" expressed as only KC can, in words only KC has. Her generosity of spirit and candid text is not a guide book or a traditional memoir. It is a reminder that every beginning is the ending of something. The transition zone of life forces needed change, creating opportunities for human growth.

KC reminds us that, while certainty is an illusion, the rewards of persistence and self-trust are resilience and inner strength. And that we are all humans who share a need to find tools, skills, tricks - whatever to avoid moral injury and remain positively engaged in life.

Thank you for writing this book at this time, my friend. Ever forward in real time.

Sherellen B Gerhart MD

Introduction

"Have the courage to face the light of your own being."

—Sufi saying

I didn't expect to fall out of love with my career any more than I expected to fall out of love with my husband.

I was deeply invested in both my marriage and my career going the distance. Neither did. In both situations, things looked great on paper, however, in practice, I wasn't ideally suited for either of them. But there I was, well into my 40s, married to a physician and living the good life in a sunny, moneyed suburb of San Francisco. I had a beautiful home, handsome accomplished husband, gorgeous kids and a thriving career working for a noble cause. What's the problem, right? In both cases it eventually became painfully obvious to me that I had ignored all sorts of red flags on my way to that charmed life. Yep, just ran right over those stop signs! It's no surprise that over time, "we" grew apart and no amount of compromise, counselling, or sheer force of will could fix my doomed marriage or my faltering career. And I'm better for accepting both of these truths.

Why?

Because those losses spurred me on and equipped me to find a better fit for myself, when it came to work *and* love.

I'm getting ahead of myself though, and it's probably best to go back to the beginning. So let's start there. Hold on for the ride.

I've always been a helper, and I entered healthcare with that objective in mind. In retrospect, though, I don't think I was ever a good match for medicine. I have a philosopher's mind (with a frequently mocked college degree to show for it) that thrives on asking the deeper questions about life for which the only answers come in muddled shades of grey. Healthcare is science (it's art, too, but that part isn't advertised as much) in which the questions have definite, clear answers. Black and white, good and bad, with strictly prescribed ways of doing things. Even though healthcare sells itself as "individualized", in practice, it rarely is. Truth. Anyhow, ignoring all these signs of a poor fit, I charged forth anyway and pursued a career in healthcare. Armed with a second bachelor's degree in nursing as well as a master's, I entered practice as an adult nurse practitioner.

It became clear early on that the more traditional (read: rigid) fields of healthcare were not for me. I wandered through and wet my feet in the areas of oncology, primary care, and geriatrics, and finally realized how much I don't thrive on absolutes and the paternalistic relationship that is often expected between provider and patient. For someone deeply invested in high falutin' dreams of promoting autonomy and shared decision making, this was not good. I wanted big ideals and instead found a sea of checkboxes, flowcharts, diagnostic codes and decision trees. Not what I signed up for. Big fucking yawn, actually.

I eventually connected with hospice and felt I'd finally found my healthcare home. Here were patients I was uniquely qualified to help with my specific skills and proclivities. If you want to speak frankly about hard things—like searching for meaning in life and exploring the possibilities regarding what comes next after...well, you know—death, then I am your girl! I love that light and fluffy stuff! All in a day's work, though, and I shined at it. I also became adept at clinical symptom management, thanks to my puzzle-loving brain and a setting in which thinking creatively is not only encouraged but often necessary when operating away from the cushy confines of the hospital or clinic. For many years, I thrived. I had great mentors, I enjoyed learning things to continually improve my practice and, over time, I became an expert.

Life was peaceful then, at least on the surface. I gave birth to two beautiful children and parenting was a dream come true; effortful but wonderful. I made many friends and enjoyed a strong sense of purpose and community. Life was pretty good. For about five years. Unfortunately, my marriage was taking a slow nose dive I was desperately trying to ignore. But the cracks were showing, our paths were diverging, and a horrible stew of ugliness was bubbling up between us. I didn't feel like I could do anything right and my anxiety was off the charts. I shut down emotionally in an effort to shield myself from constant conflict that threatened my sense of self and my worth as a human being. I was so incredibly lonely in my marriage. Lonelier than if I had actually been alone. Luckily, I had good friends to provide the emotional support I wasn't getting at home and I took comfort in the knowledge that career-wise anyway, I was still valuable, still good, still rocking it. But deep down, I felt like a failure in love.

Life went on with work highs and marriage lows as my kids grew alongside. Ten years into my career when my kids reached 7 and 8 years old, my world was turned upside down by twin tragedies. My dad and brother died three weeks apart, both totally unexpected. In one fell swoop, I'd lost two of the most important people in my life— one my mentor, the other my most trusted confidant. The year 2013 was the worst of my entire life. I was completely unmoored.

But I also felt strangely clear in a way I'd never experienced before—or since, for that matter. Like I could see through all of the bullshit of life with a laser focus trained on what really matters: loved ones, peace, joy, fulfillment. My priorities became clear as cut glass and just as sharp. There was no time to waste, all of us, any of us could die at any moment.

My marriage failed fairly quickly after that, but I slogged on with my career. At least it brought me some joy and sense of accomplishment when everything else was turning to shit. But oh, how things can change.

Once everything more or less settled after my husband and I separated (the second and final time) in 2015, I reluctantly started to acknowledge a building disillusionment with my work. No major bad events occurred, it was more of a slow, steady, falling out of love initially—just like in my marriage. No punches, no affairs, no hidden gambling debts. It was a yawning divide that was there from the beginning and had grown wider. And kept growing wider until it became ugly and painful and impossible to ignore anymore. I felt like I was danger of losing myself completely. Growing despair led to a sense of desperation which eventually gave way to epiphanies and lightbulb moments of, *I don't want to stay miserable. And I don't have to!*

In retrospect, I know that I stayed in both my marriage and my healthcare career way too long. But what can you do? Falling out of love is a process and it takes time.

And life is too short for dwelling on regrets. People learn lessons and make changes in their own time (and sometimes they don't). That being said, one of the big lessons I have learned in this process of falling out of love is the necessity of allowing a place for *all* emotions at my table, not just the pretty ones. What's the point of sitting around feeling bad, you ask? Because those uncomfortable feelings often provide very useful information. Sadness? Take a seat. Anxiety? Let me pull that chair out for you. Anger and frustration? Please sit next to me. I have come to understand that ignoring or pushing these feelings away does nothing but encourage them to come back, stronger and demanding my attention even more because they are trying to tell me something important. By allowing them to guide my attention to those painful parts of me that need healing, attention, and growth they are no longer fearsome. And the "happier" feelings let me know when I am on the right track. I give each of them, the positive and the negative, plenty of airtime right here in these pages—the whole authentic experience of leaving a calling that had gone silent, and what I learned in the process of letting go of what no longer fits.

What follows is the rest of that story. The ups, the downs, the altogether disorienting and exciting rollercoaster ride of leaving my career in healthcare for good. The slow, melancholy parts. The swift decisions and leaps of faith. Learning how to put myself first, becoming honest about what makes me tick (the good and the bad), where my talents are, and what makes me feel truly fulfilled. It's a story about finding my identity, becoming the me that's more me. The *me-er* me. Warning: it's downright awful at times and straight lines don't seem to exist in this process. It's a whole stew of emotions presented here, raw and genuine. But neatly packaged in bite-sized chapters for you, should you care to reference them while going through your own struggles. Perhaps to take comfort in the fact that someone else is slogging through similar shit. Or, alternatively, to feel superior that you're not as fucked up as I am! But hey—we're all a little fucked up, aren't we? Yes, indeed, we are.

Speaking of fucked up, I didn't write this book "by the book", so to speak. Far from it. I jumped right into the middle and wrote about my lived experience going through a major career change in real time. I didn't want to risk waiting and then looking back on that tumultuous and confusing period of my life from the safety of the solid ground of my new future and writing a bunch of revisionist bullshit about how "it wasn't really all that bad". I knew I wanted to capture a true account of how it feels falling out of love with your work, leaping off of a jagged career cliff, and hoping for the best. I wanted to describe what was going through my mind mid-flight as I hurtled through the air. So—I did that. I jumped and I wrote about all of it: the good, the not so good, and the undeniably ugly. It's sort of embarrassing now to read some of the stuff I was fretting about back then, but hey—it was real.

And when I was done writing my soul-revealing story and had put the finishing touches on what had become my book baby, I shipped it off to a very kind agent, full of hope. A few interminable days later, his response was in. To be fair, he offered *some* encouraging words, but I mostly fixated on the parts that he said didn't work. Even though none of the feedback was terrible, the thing that gutted me the most was the observation that it didn't seem like I knew what I wanted this book to be. He said that there was no clear message, no structure. Is it a memoir, is it self-help, is it philosophy? What is it? Even I wasn't sure. Maybe all three?

And, he concluded, it was way too short. Ouch.

My prickly (alright, maybe slightly irked) reaction to his critique actually ended up being a cue to myself to *pay attention*. The fact that I was upset likely meant there was some truth in his words. Damn.

But here's the thing: I wasn't willing to compromise on saying things in my own, concise way. Without filters, without bullshit, only a passing nod to grammar rules and with plenty of colorful language AKA cursing (sorry to my sister who will surely cringe). My style was not up for discussion. And the content was a faithful account of what I went through and how I made sense of it all at the time, so I wasn't willing to change that either. If it reads as slightly disjointed, that's because that's how it was experienced and documented. This was far from a clean and linear activity! But the part about needing some unifying clarity and structure for potential readers? Well, I'll grudgingly admit that he had a point there.

I suspect that many—if not most—writers figure out what they want to say *before* they actually start writing. And yup—I definitely see how that would have been way easier! But I stand by my decision to document my transition as it unfolded. Falling out of love with my career didn't happen overnight, nor did finding my new direction. It was a journey I lived and faithfully wrote about. I didn't try to control the writing; I simply allowed the words to come out of me however they did at the time.

But now the tricky part — going back and trying to figure out what it all means. Not to mention trying to stitch it together into some kind of coherent story that people might actually want to read. No big deal, right?

Huge deal. Beleaguered, and irked (again), I lamented to myself, "How the fuck am I going to do that?" Here I had perfectly delicious bite-sized cookies and the task set out before me was to somehow turn them into a cake. Best get baking.

I pondered how there is a tendency with readers and writers alike to want to move the story along from point A to point B without getting bogged down. The end is often valued more highly than the means to get there. Nobody wants to experience, or read about, a ship stuck between two shores forever. They want to know where that ship is going and what the sailors find when they get "there". This urgency often applies to those pursuing life change or writing about it as well. There are a lot of books out there about figuring out your purpose, and there's plenty of advice on how to transform your life quickly and efficiently through various generic, prescribed means. Skip that long ocean voyage – plenty of the life change gurus have a "one size fits all" plan—just for you! They say you can achieve your dreams TODAY! Don't waste any time mucking about in the "messy middle"! That's just one big flyover state getting in the way, something to be endured on the way to better things.

I think that is a damn shame.

What this disheartening encounter with the agent helped me to realize is this: anyone can live through (and write about) an experience. Even a massive, life-changing one like a career shift or, for that matter, a divorce (yup—I endured and wrote about that one, too). It's what you *do* with that experience that matters. I think for many of us, there's this expectation to grit our teeth, close our eyes, and gut out the big changes so that we can move on quickly. We want to put those difficult episodes behind us and keep our focus firmly on the future. Instead, I'm advocating for you to stop and take a look around while you're in the middle of it—whatever your "it" might be. What can you learn from the ordeal you are going through, how do you apply that wisdom, and how does it help you in this present venture and in the future? Perhaps, at the very least, it can teach you to avoid repeating the same old mistakes?

You can survive a lot of things, but taking the time to make sense out of them is what allows you to thrive going forward. So really, in retrospect, I got more out of writing this book backwards than if I'd gone the traditional route. It allowed me to see patterns and themes *after the fact* that I definitely missed while I was in the thick of it all. One of the most important things I have learned from my own adventure (and it's also the reason why you should read this book) is that there is gold in that messy middle. Go ahead and spend some quality time there, and keep your eyes open for the whole ride. See how it changes you from the inside out. Because I assure you, it will.

You can take a look right here at what happened to me when I squashed my impulse to try to control the mess and instead just let it unfold. I'll tell you what I heard when I tuned in and listened to my own internal world. To be sure, ugly stuff did come to the surface, but I refused to be sucked into a spiral of shame, discouragement, and, ultimately, defeat. I stayed alert instead of letting unhelpful reflexes take over and push away all my uncomfortable emotions. I learned a great deal—in the moment and even more afterward—including that I was more fucked up than I originally thought! But, more importantly, I also discovered that I was stronger and more resilient as well.

To be certain, concrete changes in my life happened to me externally; I now have a new career direction and this book to show for it all. But the real treasure was in what happened on the *inside*. I gathered little bits of insight along the way and uncovered even bigger things—deeply held intrinsic personal values, in fact—when I took a look back at it all from the end. If I'd rushed it, impulsively chucked my career in healthcare, and jumped into a new life as a writer all in one go I would have missed all sorts of wisdom in between. Instead, I took the time to grieve leaving my old career, to heal from the experience, learn from it, expand, and grow into my new self. This is what it takes to effectively fall out of love—with a career or with anyone or anything else. And every one of those insights I picked up along the way, whether big or little, will armor me for whatever comes down the pike in the future. Screw the life change gurus. Let your own experience be your guide. It's a wild ride, sure. But it's certainly worth it.

I hope that the readers of this book—the book that finally emerged (agent criticisms notwithstanding)—will find some comfort and inspiration here and that it will have bearing on their own major life transitions. You don't even have to be going through a career change at all. I believe the concepts I explore within these pages are relevant to any big life change—be it in terms of your career, relationships, or any other hardships you might be facing. You don't have to be miserable in healthcare or have ever worn scrubs or a white coat like me to get something inspiring out of this book. It is not healthcare specific. I promise.

Whoever and wherever you are in your life transition, consider reading this book in small doses. My intention is that these ideas are enjoyed in little bites (hence the short chapters) because I want you to really think about how these things apply (or not) to your own situation. Read this book for wisdom, for entertainment (the comedy! The drama!), for insight, or for comfort and commiseration. But above all else, read it for the inspiration to think about this stuff in relation to your own life and where and how you might go on from here. Because the only way is up. Unless, of course, the only way is down, but I want to help you fly off that jagged cliff—not plummet from it.

At the time, the experience of falling out of love with my career was a confusing and uncomfortable blur with tiny nuggets of insight and wisdom strewn here and there. However, looking back now, I see that four main principles were actually hard at work, helping steer me through:

Life is too short to be miserable.

Handle your shit.

You don't have to live your life like everyone else.

Enjoy the path.

This is the wisdom — these four deeply held personal values — that emerged for me only when I took the time to contemplate this process through the lens of hindsight. The rearview mirror can be *such* a blessing. These values were at work in the background all along, even though I was mostly unaware of them at the time. But they were there, quietly helping me navigate all the challenging steps in this journey. These guiding principles allowed me to finally achieve a dramatic and fulfilling life change, and yet it was only while reviewing the entire experience afterwards that I recognized them. Your personal principles may be different than mine; in fact, they very likely will be. But whatever they are, listen to them, and let them guide you to the *you-er* you.

No matter where I end up on this odyssey (because it's still going—and thank God for that), I am truly grateful for the lived experience of making a big change, studying myself throughout that process, and then writing about it. I've grown incredibly in so many different ways and I've become a hell of a lot more authentically me. In the end, I know myself, I understand myself, I accept my imperfect self, and I like myself a whole lot better now. With or without external success as a writer, this journey has been worth every minute. And I'd do it all over again.

"You don't get to choose how you are going to die or when. You can only decide how you are going to live. Now."

—Joan Baez, American singer-songwriter

Part 1: Life is Too Short to Be Miserable

Falling Out of Love

It's hard to pinpoint precisely when I fell out of love with my healthcare career. Just like with my first husband, I don't think we were ever a match made in heaven. I think that in both cases I settled for "good enough" instead of being braver and pursuing "great". But I was ready to commit, dammit! I was ready to get on with having a "real" career when I did (in my late 20s) and I was ready to get married and have a family when I did (in my early 30s). I was tired of striving; I wanted some *arriving*.

And I was reasonably happy with my career and my marriage, until I wasn't. Very likely, there had been signs that we were drifting apart, but I didn't see them because I didn't want to. That seems to be a familiar story for most people. I was heavily invested in living the life that was expected of me. Not just expected of me from others either, but also from *myself*. And that vision included a lifelong marriage and a successful career doing "good work". Fairytale, right? Rare is the person who can't relate to wanting that kind of perceived success.

There were flashes of clarity about the problems in my marriage and career that eventually turned into persistent feelings of discontent in my life. However, separating from my husband and leaving my job were not fast or easy tasks. Falling out of love in both cases was messy, painful, and disorienting.

But I knew an end to that mélange of misery was possible. And it was up to me to make it happen.

Life is too short to be miserable.

Disappointment

Disappointment: *sadness or displeasure caused by the nonful-fillment of one's hopes or expectations*

"If we will be quiet and ready enough, we shall find compen-sation in every disappointment."

—Henry David Thoreau, American poet

My career in healthcare was born from disappointment. As early as I can remember, seeing the doctor was an experience that left me cold, and sometimes worse off than before. As a child, we had an early forerunner of an HMO-style system in which I never saw "my" doctor, or even the same doctor twice. As I was an introvert (and often mislabeled as shy), this was not the ideal set-up for a satisfying patient experience. I need to observe people for a while before letting them into my world fully, and I've been that way since I was a child. So being treated by a different doctor each and every time left me feeling like I was twisting in the wind, never securely moored, never known, understood, or cared for. Luckily, I was a healthy kid, so I didn't require much contact beyond unpleasant an-nual check-ups, bouts of strep throat, and a particularly nasty sprained ankle acquired on the tennis team in high school while booking it cross-court to return a blazing backhand. I don't recall if I made the shot, but I like to think that I did.

That all changed when I went away to college at the University of California, Berkeley. I had access to the student health center staffed largely by nurse practitioners (known in the industry as NPs). I had never been treated by an NP before, and it was a revelation. Who were these angels who made me feel seen, heard, and known? No major health issues, mind you—just garden variety stuff—but for the first time ever, I felt what it was like to receive honest to goodness *care*. Good care, thorough care, helpful care. These encounters affected the course of my whole life. For this experience led me away from my initial plan to study law and toward a career in healthcare, where I hoped I could make a similar impact on other people's lives in a direct, meaningful, personal way.

I kept my major in philosophy, but also began taking science courses. Yikes! I'd been the kid in high school who skipped calculus because I was *so sure* that I would not need it in my career path. Ha! Blew that one. It was painful and difficult to shift my mind away from words and ideas toward cold, hard facts and numbers. My GPA certainly took a hit, but I was determined to walk this path and become an NP. After graduation, I joined AmeriCorps and taught reading to inner city kids in Seattle to help earn money for further study. I took classes at community college to finish the rest of my science prerequisites for nursing school, finally transferring into Seattle University to finish my second bachelor's degree in nursing. I cannot say enough glowing things about my two years there. I had great mentors at that institution who inspired me to try new things, like traveling to Belize for a school term to provide in-home care to seniors through a charity clinic, and working as a nursing aide for hospice patients. Both were life affirming and career affirming experiences; I felt like I was definitely on the right track. Two and a half years later, I was a brand new RN with my sights set on graduate school to become an NP. But first, I needed some patient experience. I worked at the Veteran's hospital in Seattle on the oncology ward and then for a local hospice. Both were great experiences and I found I felt very at home with end of life care.

Next stop was the University of Washington, where I pursued my master's degree in their homecare nurse practitioner pathway. Working part-time and studying full-time was no picnic, but thank God I love learning and am naturally wired for school. That made it manageable. Nine years of post-secondary education, many clinical rotations, and two certification exams plus the Graduate Record Examinations later, I finally arrived at my destination. I was a full-fledged adult nurse practitioner, ready for my career to begin.

Life is too short to be miserable.

Disillusionment

Disillusionment: *the condition of being dissatisfied or defeated in expectation or hope*

"Wisdom comes by disillusionment."

—George Santayana, Spanish-American philosopher

Unfortunately, it didn't take long for disillusionment to show up in my brand-new career. I'd studied in Washington state, but I had my sights set on sunny California. Visions of breezy warmth, clear skies and sun-kissed dreams beckoned and my soon-to-be husband and I answered the call. It was a shock to learn upon arrival that, unlike in Washington where I'd trained, California has significant restrictions on NP practice, including requiring a "collaborating physician" arrangement. I must have been out sick the day we learned in school that laws governing NP practice vary from state to state. This is not what I signed up for! I expected to be independent, a master of my own world but was greeted with a leash. *Well, nothing to do but to get on with it.* Later I learned that in practice these restrictions didn't amount to much other than bureaucracy and paperwork, but that's California for you. I might have a "collaborating physician", but it was still my license and my ass on the line when providing care.

I got my first job working with a pair of doctors doing super interesting, cutting-edge radiation treatments for patients with certain types of cancer. It felt...well, important. It was cool to learn new stuff, I loved the patient interactions, and, in addition to my other responsibilities, I found a niche for myself creating patient education materials. There was no consistent process in place to help people understand the treatment options being offered and I felt it was important to do my part to try to fix that. This was fulfilling, but in time the tension-filled relationship between the doctor partners and the megalomania of the guy who founded the practice led me to look for something else. I didn't want to be part of their harried scene forever.

I soon shifted gears and started working in elder care. I've always loved and respected older people, so it felt like a great fit. The work was good and I felt like I was performing a needed service for a traditionally underserved population. But the company who employed me and farmed out my services to these patients was poorly run—and possibly also a bit shady. The company ended up leaving practice in the state of California and laying me off when I was eight-months pregnant. Honestly, I didn't mind.

Luckily, I had taken a side gig with a local hospice before I was let go from my full-time gig and they were eager to make me a full-time employee. After my baby was born, I took them up on that offer and I was happy there for a large chunk of my career. I felt like I was finally in the right field at the right company. End of life care allowed me to integrate my philosophy background with my clinical skills, which made me feel complete. It was a respectful environment. I had great mentors there. Work was stimulating, fulfilling, and fun. I felt accomplished, like I'd hit my stride. But sadly (and inevitably, I suppose), this is also when my marriage first started to hit the skids. The stress of being parents, even though a welcome and wonderful duty, exposed all the cracks in our relationship. As our kids grew up, we grew further apart but continued to soldier on.

I was abruptly shaken out of my complacency when my dad and brother died suddenly in the spring of 2013. My dad, my trusted mentor, had turned 75 shortly beforehand. He was uber healthy and, ironically, died on his way to the starting line of the Big Sur International Marathon. I was there at the coast with my children to cheer him on. My mom and I we were driving the kids around in Monterey, looking for fun and adventure when the bottom fell out from our world. I'll never forget my mom hanging up the phone, turning to me and saying "your daddy is dead".

Shock set in, alleviated only by obligatory busyness; I took on the task of alerting the family. Aunts, uncles, friends, siblings. All except for my older brother, Mike. He was there doing the same marathon and was unreachable on the course. We had to wait until he finished to break the terrible news to him.

In the sea of smiling, happy people greeting their loved ones with pride and joy at the finish line, we were the incongruent grey ones. My mom and I, with my kids in tow, could barely contain our grief. Mike finally arrived—flushed, happy, and full of good-natured bluster about our perpetually late dad's failure to connect with him on the course. It was one of the worst moments of my life when I had to tell him why dad hadn't show up to meet him. Obviously, the news absolutely crushed him. The rest of us, too. Our dad was a patriarch, in every positive sense of the word. Our close-knit, loving, safe family suddenly had a big, gaping hole in it.

My other siblings flew in from all directions and the family gathered in beautiful Monterey that night. The planned post-race celebration went ahead, with an empty place at the head of the table. We didn't know what else to do, other than to cling together in our shared shock and grief. When the details were handled, Mike and I and our sister drove our mom home to Washington—twelve hours in the car. Mostly silent up front, where my siblings took turns driving, and active in the back, where mom and I set about the business you have to take care of after someone dies. We couldn't bear to just sit with our misery; we felt compelled to stay busy. I stayed with mom for a week, sleepwalking through the days, cleaning out stuff and reading dad's journals through the nights. He'd been a prolific writer. Even though it felt a little naughty to pore over his private thoughts, I am so glad that I did. It was a chance to feel close to him for just a little bit longer. To indulge myself in his wisdom one more time and appreciate his take on the world. I am certain my deep-thinking bent is thanks to him (he always encouraged it). The family let me write his obituary. It was cathartic. We survivors, the ones left behind, cried a lot, both together and separately. Mike cooked our old family favorites (he was a classically trained chef, but definitely not above the comforting allure of meatloaf and navy bean soup). It was painstaking to even think about returning to normal life, but one of my kids back at home in California with my husband had gotten sick and duty called.

A semblance of normal life resumed until only three weeks later, I received the 3 a.m. phone call everyone dreads. My adored, handsome, charming, older brother, Mike—my best friend—had died in his sleep. No explanations, no foul play. He just died for no apparently good reason at all. Other than maybe a broken heart, as he and dad had been close. I mean *really* close.

My husband and I got in the car in the dark of the early morning with the kids bundled up in the back. An hour on the road passed that I don't even remember. It was still dark outside when my husband dropped me off at Mike's house to help my sister-in-law. Still reeling from dad's death, we began the whole excruciating notification and grieving process all over again.

I consider myself a capable communicator, but I can't even find the words—still—to illustrate how much this gutted me. It sucked. And it sucked every breath of wind out of my sails.

I was angry at Mike for leaving me alone to deal with the mess of dad's death and now his own. I was heartbroken, lonely, and just plain devastated by these two sudden and unexpected losses. Nothing made sense anymore. It's like somebody had come in and rearranged all the furniture and turned out the lights, leaving me to stumble around in the dark while shepherding my mom and surviving siblings through a total nightmare. I felt numb to my bones but also crackling with sensation. This was real life, and it doesn't get much realer.

I didn't know a person could have so many tears. And I hid them. Or tried to, from my young kids especially, so as not to completely freak them out. And also from my husband, because he just couldn't be bothered. I had been feeling alone and lonely in my marriage for some time and the gulf between us yawned even wider through these events. I sensed my devastating grief was nothing more than another annoyance to him, another way I had become a burden and a bane of his happiness.

I grieved hard, for a solid year. I took to walking alone around the Lafayette Reservoir trail in the early mornings. A two-and-a-half-mile path around a sparkling blue lake, tucked into sunbaked hills that were either toasty brown or vibrant green depending on the season. I spent this time crying my eyes out behind the shield of my sunglasses in the bright, northern California summer mornings, or in the cold, inky, private blackness of the winter ones. I felt like a crazy woman. This was primal, visceral pain that needed to come out, and this was when and where I ended up releasing it. When those hour-long marches were over, it was back into Mom and Mrs. mode—and back to my profession of caring for other people's dying loved ones while deeply missing my own and trying to figure out how my life made sense without them.

However, I was so grateful to be surrounded and supported by my hospice colleagues during that awful time. They knew how to comfort and support me in my devastating grief when no one else seemed to have a clue about what to say or do. But the light never came back on for me—not in my marriage and not in my career. I didn't realize it at the time, but the experience of those deaths was a sentinel event that profoundly changed the course of my life. Not immediately, but in both ways, decidedly for the better.

While in the depths of my grief, I had a sudden clarity and profound shift in my internal GPS that reordered my priorities. I'd always felt like I had things in good order before, but certain ideas took on a whole new poignancy. They became visceral knowing as opposed to mere abstract thoughts: *life can be fucking unpredictable. Life is too short, too long, too valuable* (depends on your perspective) *to be miserable. Too short if you are putting off doing things you really want to do, like pursuing the work of your dreams or spending time with the people you love or finding the love of your life. Too painfully long when you are slogging away in a job or marriage that don't fit you. Too valuable to waste it on shit that doesn't matter.* These insights led me to get honest with myself: I didn't trust my husband with my heart and was deeply unhappy and unfulfilled in my marriage. I was not fulfilled in my work either and both of these things drained me emotionally to the point that I was not present for the truly important people and parts of my life.

My work experiences during the years that followed saw their highs and lows. I was still at that lovely little independent hospice, but change was afoot. I stayed for nearly 10 years altogether before the entire senior leadership of the company changed over in a short space of time, and it wasn't nearly as idyllic anymore. The bubble had burst. The culture that had made it great was systematically rooted out. That said, it's still the main job I think of when I want to remember the high points of my career. I can be confident knowing that I did a lot of good there.

The loss of my workplace of bliss and growing distaste for my career in general led to a series of bad jobs. There was the absolutely dismal time when I accepted a position at a hospital to anchor their brand new pilot program for inpatient palliative care. This felt like an exciting career step and a wonderful new challenge for me, however, I was not welcomed with open arms. Even though I think NPs are amazing, competent, and wonderful, not everyone else does. Many (but not all) physicians treat us as second-class citizens. Some patients do, too. Add that to the fact that the title includes "nurse", which many people just can't see beyond. Don't get me wrong—I was proud to be a nurse at the beginning of my working life and it *is* a wonderful career. However, as an NP, I do very little traditional nursing stuff. So to lump me in with other nurses is doing a disservice to my profession, skills, and education. I hope that doesn't sound strident, but the difference matters. I am also not a "physician extender" or "almost a doctor" or a "mid-level provider". I am a fully trained, licensed, medical professional with a well-defined scope of practice. And it is my ass, and license, on the line for any clinical decisions I make. It is not all about titles, although they can confer a certain level of professional respect (or disrespect, as the case may be). The old boys club of physicians at the hospital were unwelcoming and downright rude at times. This is unverified, and don't quote me, but the scuttlebutt was that they had a long-held stance that "No NP will ever darken the doorstep of this hospital during our tenure." Sounds about right based on what I experienced there; I lasted three months.

That gem of a job was followed by the soul-numbing experience I had at a hospice attached to a larger health system. They had restrictions on my practice as an NP that went far beyond what the state required. Why? Not sure. This essentially reduced me to performing regulatory visits—and that was it (just a shit job they needed done by an NP for compliance). I stayed, even though my brain was turning to mush because I was still busy with grieving my dad and brother and struggling to survive in my rapidly deteriorating marriage. Finding a better job was low on the priority list at that time.

Hoping for a fresh start, my husband and I moved back to Washington state where our marriage proceeded to fully implode within a few months. Newly divorced (not exactly the fresh start I had anticipated), I started another succession of jobs which included a whole variety of settings. I had hope of renewed career vigor with each one, but none delivered. There was the time I taught medical science in high school. Working with the kids was (mostly) a joy, but the clinical rotations in the nursing home were torture. Not because I was spending long hours with self-absorbed teenagers trying to train them to be responsible caregivers with variable success (although that sure didn't help), but because I saw firsthand the way we, as a society, treat our elderly. And it is so unbelievably messed up. Warehousing older people in institutions where the sum total of healthcare they receive often amounts to a required monthly "visit" (which may be simply a wave from the doorway) from their provider. Disgusting. Major stuff was getting missed, too, often resulting in yet another frail, old person getting shipped off to the hospital for something that well could have (and should have) been prevented. And later emerging from the hospital (if they emerged) weaker and debilitated. So sad.

I moved on and took a turn in homebased primary care. I was keen on this new mission to help vulnerable, homebound old people, and the idea of caring for patients a bit upstream from hospice sounded like a positive change and a new mission I could feel good about. In practice, it sucked. Big time. It was like trying to put a bandage on a gunshot wound. So much need, so few resources, and me rarely feeling good about what care I was able to provide because it was never *enough*. Also, patients and their families were not shy about complaining and questioning and always wanting more. Most of the time, though, I couldn't blame them.

So back to hospice land I went. Something familiar sounded comforting and being back in Washington with full-practice authority again was certainly an improvement over my California experiences. Unfortunately, it soon became clear that I'd inadvertently picked a terrible organization. And I use the word "organization" very loosely, because it was anything but. Lack of infrastructure, bullying from the top management positions, ongoing staffing problems contributing to risky patient care, whimsical restrictions, and an overall view that healthcare workers are simply interchangeable cogs in the machine. Expendable. Disposable. And this was a faith-based organization! To be honest, being a provider there was frightening. I was the one who would get the calls in the middle of the night when shit went awry with patients as a result of poor management during the day. In the nocturnal hours, I often wouldn't have what or who I needed to clean up the mess. I couldn't do the job in a way that met my own internal standard for quality. That was a bitter pill to swallow and my anxiety was sky-high, through the roof while working there.

It was disheartening in general to keep discovering these sorts of intrinsic problems with jobs that are tricky, if not impossible, to suss out from the other side of the interview table. You don't know you are going to hate working at a new place until you are already several months in. So what do you do? Stick it out for at least a year to maintain appearances or find a new job and suck up the gap in your resume? Neither is very palatable and I've done it both ways. All of this being said, from discussions with colleagues in other institutions, I think things are just mighty tough for everyone in healthcare, no matter where they work.

Incredibly disillusioned and burned out, I made my first departure from full time employment in April 2019. To keep solvent, I gathered multiple part-time jobs in everything from curriculum development to wound care. Anything to avoid another soul-destroying career-level job. I scrambled around making money in dribs and drabs until succumbing to the lure of the steady paycheck and returning to full-time hospice work. I lasted just over a year before jumping ship for the last time in October 2022.

I still needed money though, so I took a flexible job performing health risk assessments on a per diem basis. These are sometimes called "annual wellness visits" and are covered by Medicare and other insurance providers. The job involves reviewing patients' health history and conducting an exam to identify any gaps in care or knowledge deficits and then referring them back to their own provider for follow-up. I was ready and relieved to be off the hook of clinical responsibility in that job. However, seeing first hand how easily fragile patients can fall through the cracks was hard to bear. It was shocking how many of these folks were on my visit list, specifically because they hadn't been receiving regular care. In some cases, I was the first provider they had seen in over 20 years! But they didn't receive "regular care" for a whole host of reasons: fear of potential costs, actual costs, inability to find a provider who was covered by their insurance, disappointment with care received (leading to avoidance), scarcity of providers available, frequent turnover of personnel in clinics and sometimes a deep distrust of healthcare in general. I did my best to be kind, caring, and informative, but it was hard to see such bad and non-existent healthcare out there. And the knowledge gaps! Stunning. And terrifying. I'm not totally naïve; I realize that in many cases, patients do not retain the information they are told, and often fail or choose not to follow our advice. That's just the way it goes, and I am definitely not trying to denigrate the efforts of my provider colleagues here. We are all horribly constrained by the system of healthcare that's evolved in this country. And there is *a lot* wrong with how our system treats the people we're trying to help, as well as those of us attempting to provide that care. It becomes impossible for any of us to succeed.

I lay much of this mess at the feet of insurance providers, the ones actually in charge of this shit show. They determine what gets paid for and, therefore, what gets done in most cases. Not many patients can afford to go rogue and pay out of pocket for stuff that isn't covered by their plan. So that means that very important aspects of your care -which providers you can see, what for and when, what tests they can order, and what drugs and treatments are covered - are all ultimately determined by your insurance carrier. And there are so many different insurance plans, each with different formularies, coverages, copays, and so on. It is an absolute nightmare for patients seeking care. Navigating all of that as a provider is similarly fraught, but we must also try to be present, caring, and ultimately to do a good job—all in a 10- or 15-minute-long visit. And don't mess up your billing codes, because then you won't get paid at all (under the current coding system of 2023, there are over 70,000 procedure codes and 69,000 diagnosis codes to choose from). It is damn near impossible not to lose your mind. Or at least your commitment. Christ, I know I did.

So not only was I disillusioned with my role in healthcare, but I was becoming increasingly disillusioned with the American healthcare system in general. My own experience as a patient contributed to that, as well as the plight of my mother, now in her 80s with chronic health conditions. I've long given up on trying to receive good care for myself through the usual channels, and instead pay out of pocket to get the care that I need from a naturopath. Yep, I've gone full-on woo-woo. Not really, but I just want someone to take the time to listen and genuinely partner with me, instead of going off of a generic playbook devised by my insurance company. I have found that the "alternative" medicine providers do a much better job of actually "caring" for me.

However, my mom is a little more traditional in these matters, so I often end up riding along with her to her healthcare appointments to listen and advocate. Make no mistake: I have no intention of meddling in my mom's care and making things difficult for her providers. I know how hard that job is. In fact, I very much do *not* want to be her provider—backseat or otherwise! However, I'm aware that our healthcare system sucks and, therefore, I want to be there to stand up for my mom and try to help her avoid as many pitfalls as possible. Those cracks in the system be wide, let me tell you. Here's a sampling of ways I have helped her avoid problems: advising her not to fill a prescription for a "new" medication that was actually the generic version for one she was already on (taking both would have been a double dose of the same drug and could have, at best, been completely unnecessary, and, at worst, caused a harmful overdose). Or reining in hospital staff when they wanted to go off script and ignore mom's expressed and documented wishes about treatments she doesn't want. Re-emphasizing her listed allergies when her provider wanted to start her on a related medication. Helping her understand that while over the counter medications are available for anyone to buy, they aren't always safe. Guiding her in what and how to effectively ask for specific equipment, treatments, and services that she needs. Telling her when she should really go to urgent care or the ER and not mess around with any delays trying to get help from her overly busy primary care provider. And don't even get me started on the insurance clarification duties I do for her. The one that really breaks my heart over and over, though, is when I have to caution her that rather than assuming her multiple providers are communicating with each other, she instead should assume that they are not. She desperately wants our system to work! She wants healthcare to be good and reliable since she's so incredibly vulnerable, but, bless her heart, it just isn't. It's a minefield—often filled with jaded people who got into the business for the right reasons, but have since burned out and lost their compassion along the way. That's what happens when you spend day after day at work, overwhelmed by the health needs of the public and a system that does not provide.

My mom is one of the lucky ones too—she is white, speaks English, has health insurance, has money, and she has me. But what happens to the people who don't have these kinds of advantages? Who looks after all this risk management, advocacy, and education for people without a medical person in the family? No one, that's who. As a result, errors, oversights, mistakes, bad outcomes, and deep dissatisfaction occur—and are, in fact, rampant. And that's when you're privileged enough to have health insurance. Those without it or who are underinsured because of the expense of paying insurance premiums and copays out of pocket (that's me, self-employed, right here) struggle to find and pay for care.

And even with coverage or money, good luck finding a provider who accepts new patients. Yet plenty of Americans persist in hollowly (and grossly incorrectly) proclaiming our healthcare system to be world class. USA, yay! What a bunch of hogwash.

I was discouraged when a move back to Washington, a divorce, and several more job changes did not alleviate my disillusionment with my career. If anything, these things just cemented the malaise. I started out in my career with big dreams and noble intentions. I have been chewed up and spit out by the American healthcare system. Like many providers, and patients, before me. I am done.

Life is too short to be miserable.

Denial

Denial: *refusal to admit the truth or reality of something*

"Acknowledging that there's something you desire, not going after it, and deciding that, 'You know what, it's fine; I'll just focus on what I do have, make myself a ham sandwich, and call it a day', isn't happiness. It's denial."

—Jen Sincero, American writer

Denial, for me, was centered around the truths about my marriage and my career that I didn't want to see. Neither one was working, but to admit that felt like an overwhelming defeat. It became easier (for a while) to deny that both were falling apart. The status quo was known and familiar, and I was comfortable in my dissatisfaction and misery, even though I was terribly unhappy.

On some level, my denial also allowed me to maintain hope. Hope for improvement, and hope that things would get better without me having to make any big scary changes in either domain. I told myself that maybe my then husband and I just needed a few counseling sessions or a move to a new city for a fresh start to fix our marriage. If I was happier in my marriage, surely that would lead to more satisfaction in my career, right?

But like a sliver festering under the skin, these truths could not be denied forever.

My marriage disintegrated first. When I finally stepped out from behind my shield of denial, I felt a strange peace come over me. The cost of staying married had become too high and something else—anything else—would surely be better. So I took the leap.

I'd like to say it was all sunshine and roses after making the big decision to end my marriage, but that would be denial, too. It was horrendous. I felt like a failure. And to compound that feeling, as a newly single mom, I felt even more trapped in my loveless career. I tried to practice gratitude for having a solid profession to support myself and my family. I tried to ignore how unhappy I felt and that I dreaded going to work each day. I went through the same bargaining process with myself as when I was trying to "save" my marriage: *I'll get a new job, a new specialty. Maybe I'll try teaching, or just work less*—anything to stay in my career and make it go the distance 'til retirement. But just like with my marriage, nothing worked. I felt like a leaf caught in a swirling eddy, unable to move forward or back. My career and I simply no longer fit together and we were stuck in a bad place.

Even though I wasn't prepared to fully accept this reality yet, I did finally get around to asking myself what I really, *really* wanted to do with the rest of my life. It was here that I found yet another pristine, untapped vein of denial. Writers are rockstars in my world, but admitting that my dream was to be one myself felt like a bridge too far. I'd been doing some hobby writing on the side, but nothing serious, and certainly nothing with earning potential. *Better to settle for less*, I told myself. *Something that feels more attainable.* To this ill-advised end, I started a healthcare consulting business. My thinking was that maybe if I was self-employed, it would solve my career problems and I wouldn't have to completely waste my education and experience. I set about cherry-picking the parts of healthcare work that I felt I could tolerate and also targeted some of the most offensive holes in the system, as I saw them. I put my puzzle-loving, process-improvement oriented brain to work and devised my plan. I would be an advocate for those who needed an experienced guide to receive effective care from a broken American healthcare system. Patients were getting lost and I was uniquely suited to help them find their way. A great idea, a noble purpose, but my heart was never in it, not even from the get-go. I deluded myself and "reasoned" that I could get the business off the ground and then delegate all the operations to someone else so I wouldn't have to do it anymore. Not exactly a recipe for success, but off I went, merrily down that rabbit hole and wrapped in my warm cloak of denial. Denial and I had become best fucking friends, but, truth be told, he was becoming tiresome.

Life is too short to be miserable.

Despair

Despair: *the complete loss or absence of hope*

"Transformation is a process, and as life happens there are tons of ups and downs. It's a journey of discovery—there are moments on mountaintops and moments in deep valleys of despair."

—Rick Warren, American author

No matter how hard I tried to distract myself and "make it work", despair about my healthcare career became ever-present and unavoidable. I was fucking miserable at work! I went from competent and fulfilled to feeling like work was a collar and leash —and then a noose around my neck— slowly choking the life from me. Maybe that sounds melodramatic, but in my darkest days, I felt pretty hopeless. I didn't see any way I could stay in my career, but didn't feel like I had any other viable ways to keep making money to support my family, either.

As with most emotions, this one didn't last forever, but it was definitely impossible to ignore. Ultimately, it forced me to figure out some sort of a new direction that didn't make me feel like I was slowly dying.

So I decided to let myself dare to dream of a different career.

Despair is stubborn, though.

At the center of all my dreaming big and visualizing my future as a "writer of wisdom and wit" is a solid pit of despair. It's like a deep, deep knowing that, at some point, I will be forced to return to healthcare work in order to survive.

Gah! So awful. Trapped — this feeling is the epitome of despair to me.

I think my hard kernel of despair has been given life by a persistent voice inside that tells me that work must be hard and unpleasant. Where did this idea even *come* from? Of course, everyone always points the finger at their parents about this stuff, but I don't think I can blame them for this (other things, though? Sure). They definitely preached the American value of the importance and necessity of hard work, but I think this ideal somehow got twisted around in my own head and became intertwined with drudgery.

Oh, believe me—I *do* know how fucked up this sounds! But here I am in a pit of despair, because I do not believe, at a core level, that I will *ever* be able to escape my healthcare career. There, I said it. This dream of being a writer is just that—a dream, a fantasy. The real world and its real work are a cold, joyless slog.

I'm not going to try to give this a silver lining for you. This isn't a chirpy, ever positive, "you can do it!" manual about how to easily succeed in reaching your dreams if you just put your mind to it. This is a real, honest description of what the experience of falling out of love with my career has been like for me. And sometimes, it's godawful. Sometimes it uncovers some deep shit, like this bogus belief that all work is hell. That's one engrained piece of garbage that needs rooting out before I can keep moving forward. Is it helpful to face this crap head on? Yes, because this is what growth is. Is it pleasant? No, it feels terrible!

But I'm going to do it anyway, because as long as this shitty despair lingers, I'll never really believe that I can have a different career and a different life.

Life is too short to be miserable.

Shame

Shame: *a painful feeling of humiliation or distress caused by the consciousness of wrong or foolish behavior*

"An exciting and inspiring future awaits you beyond the noise in your mind—beyond the guilt, doubt, fear, shame, insecurity, and heaviness of the past you carry around."

—Debbie Ford, American author

To be clear, this definition is incomplete, at least in the way I wish to use it to address how shame has affected me on this journey. It's missing the part that says that shame is in the eye of the beholder—and sometimes, that's also me. What defines "wrong or foolish behavior" is really a matter of opinion. Just because I'm living my life outside the norm does not mean I deserve to be shamed for it. But alas, people still try to shame me. And I am often one of them. Fucking traitor to my own cause is what I am! But I'm human, and humans are a bit, well...messed up.

There's been lots of shame in this journey, from all directions:

Shame from my former husband for giving my own needs, wants, or desires any level of priority during our marriage.

Shame from my own journal. *"I'm not walking my own talk about life being short—too short to be miserable and too short not to pursue dreams."* Ugh. Shaming myself!

But leaving a good paycheck and a "secure" job feels irresponsible and, thus, shameful.

Shame from my teenagers who don't want me to stick out, and who would rather I just be "normal" (in other words, just like everyone else).

Shame from my financial advisor for not having a regular full-time job.

Shame from potential employers for my checkered career path.

Shame from myself (again!) for conforming to a marriage, a lifestyle, and a career that made me miserable for so long.

Shame from society for not fitting in, for not accepting and being grateful for the life I had that we've all been taught to desire and strive for.

Shame from that stupid urgent care doc when I (briefly) did not have health insurance and unwisely broke my ankle.

In summary, shame is a fucking endless rainbow, but comes in four main shades of grey for me:

Not pursuing my dreams (sooner).

Leaving a perfectly secure and lucrative career.

Not living my life as expected.

Living my life as expected.

To put it another way: damned if I do, damned if I don't.

And the quote that begins this section? I purposely picked it for its sunny outlook, a rich counterpoint to the dour definition. It gives me some welcome hope that I will eventually move beyond shame and into a healthy acceptance. I'm certainly not there yet; I still care way too much about what people think. It is hard to admit that. And guess what? I feel shame about that too! But being honest with myself about this has brought it into the light where I can see these words written on the page and appreciate how messed up they are (as I am; trust me, I'm the first one to admit it). The ridiculousness of all this is hard to miss. What I *have* gained thus far from plumbing the depths of my own shame, however, is the realization of how unhelpful shame is to growth and, at the same time, the necessity and possibility of letting it go.

Life is too short to be miserable.

Anxiety

Anxiety: *a feeling of worry, nervousness, or unease typically about an imminent event or something with an uncertain outcome*

"Every tomorrow has two handles. We can take hold of it with the handle of anxiety or the handle of faith."

—Henry Ward Beecher, American clergyman and speaker

Anxiety comes in all kinds of forms for me. My brain is a veritable smorgasbord of anxiety. Here's just a wee glimpse into the things that have plagued me (and some of them still do), in no particular order.

Society definitely smiles upon married people, so when I became an unmarried person again, I was hurtled right back into that pit of anxious disappointment shared by many singles. Back to feeling somehow intrinsically defective for not having (or being able to keep) a partner—and so desperate to change that. To get coupled up again (STAT!) so that I could regain the feeling of the sunlight of approval on my face and ditch the anxiety of being untethered, adrift.

When I quit my full-time job, I felt a similar sort of anxiety. I actually made myself physically sick from the desperation of figuring out my new path and reaching success as soon as humanly possible. I craved being a stable, productive, and acceptable member of working society again. As a means to manage my anxiety about how murky my future was, I started to plan. In earnest, I put together a rigid writing schedule for myself, punctuated by multiple "freelance" healthcare gigs to assuage my concurrent catastrophic worry about finances.

The money stuff was a huge hurdle for me (and still is—I'm trying to grow, though!). It's interesting to me how out of proportion my fear of guaranteed, immediate, and irreversible poverty was to the actual health of my financial state. My money situation at that time was actually pretty good. Debt was minimal (mortgage only), a rainy-day fund was in place, college and retirement savings were in good shape, we had a roof over our heads, and I had marketable skills to make money without working full time. Yet I still felt like we were *this close* to living on the street. My money anxiety wasn't based in reality, but it was oh so real. I have a feeling that some of you can relate to this—and if you can't, count me all shades of envious!

Aside from the fear of looming abject poverty, I was also anxious about taking risks, especially financial ones, to benefit myself. I was strongly and weirdly uncomfortable with making my own happiness a priority. Sounds more than a bit like motherhood there, doesn't it?

I realize it's possible that my money anxiety was (and could be) really just a cover, a convenient excuse not to work toward my dreams—and possibly fail. Which is itself yet another side of our good old friend anxiety!

I also get anxious when I'm stalled creatively, even though I understand that this ebb-and-flow pattern is part of the process. But still, what if inspiration never comes back?

Then there's the anxiety about not working hard enough. This one is a real mindfuck. I tell myself that writing doesn't feel painful or difficult or unpleasant enough to be worthwhile or profitable. It's my own twisted belief that I picked up somewhere along the way, the belief that work and success both require suffering. How lame is that?

Which leads us to: anxiety about the (lack of) quality of my writing. Self-explanatory.

This little round-up wouldn't be complete if I didn't mention my anxiety about my anxiety. Yep, worrying about being anxious. *It feels so weak to admit how much anxiety I have – everyone is going to think I am really fucked up. Wait...am I really fucked up?*

Gimme a minute and I'll probably think of more, but that's a pretty good sample of the kinds of anxiety that have wracked and riddled me. And none of it was doing anything to make me feel happy, content, or motivated. It felt like a pot of unprocessed, raw sewage stinking up my mind.

Life is too short to be miserable.

Doubt

Doubt: *a feeling of uncertainty or lack of conviction*

"We're our own worst enemy. You doubt yourself more than anybody else ever will. If you can get past that, you can be successful."

—Michael Strahan, American journalist and TV personality

What is doubt all about?

Well, I can tell you this: doubting my writing ability is not helpful to the creative process, that's for damn sure. Questioning the value of every word I put down is downright paralyzing.

Doubt has value, though, or it wouldn't exist. I believe it's there in some measure to shield my weak little ego. *I'll doubt myself first so nobody else can get the drop on me.* If I call myself out early on the fact that I'm going to fail as a writer, then I save face in some weird, twisted, fucked up way by beating others to the punch.

Doubt is trying to protect me by convincing me not to go all in on my dreams. Doubt says, "You're not good enough to make it, so don't invest yourself there." Doubt allows me an out. If

I never try my hardest, then I can at least fall back on that as an excuse when I fail.

Then I don't have to accept that my best just wasn't good enough, because I didn't *give* it my best. Doubt is insulation against the shame of trying my absolute hardest and failing. Doubt keeps me stuck. Yuck.

Life is too short to be miserable.

Melancholy

Melancholy: *a feeling of pensive sadness*

"All changes, even the most longed for, have their melancholy; for what we leave behind us is a part of ourselves; we must die to one life before we can enter another."

—Anatole France, French poet

You know, it's a shame. Just a big, fat, crying shame. So much time and life I spent pursuing a dream that no longer resonates with me. All those years of school, the drive, the desire to be somebody—somebody I no longer recognize.

Did I make a mistake in my original career choice?

Maybe, but I don't regret it. It was mostly a good chapter, but it is over now. I have changed in intrinsic ways and am no longer the same woman who made those career choices way back then.

It's kind of like after my first pregnancy. A lot about my body changed during that process, including, most surprisingly to me, my shoe size. I expected the stretch marks, the hips, the boobs, but *my feet*? And now, metaphorically at least, so many beautiful shoes no longer fit because I am a different person than I was before I was transformed by this experience.

Sometimes I feel a bit wistful. Sometimes I wish those shoes and that career still fit. Sometimes I feel a sense of sadness and loss for all that time, effort, and history that I'm letting go of.

There was a time when I did have love and passion for my work. It would be so much easier to rekindle the flame and stay, but that is simply futile now. I've tried. It's hard to accept sometimes that it really is over, and I have some transient sadness about that. Not enough to entice me to stay and keep trying, but enough to make me feel a bit gloomy on some days.

Life is too short to be miserable.

Resentment

Resentment: *bitter indignation at having been treated unfairly*

"For years I bore the crippling weight of anger, bitterness and resentment toward those who caused my suffering. Yet as I look back over a spiritual journey that has spanned more than 3 decades, I realize the same bombs that caused so much pain and suffering also brought me to a place of great healing."

—Phan Thi Kim Phuc, South Vietnamese Canadian peace activist

Resentment actually lit a fire under my ass to seek something better, both in my career and in my love life. I'm grateful for that resentment! In fact, all the words in this chapter could fit equally well under the one about Gratitude in Part 4. I enjoy talking about the "power" of resentment, though, since most people focus on how bad and awful it is for you. Don't get me wrong—long-held resentment is absolute poison, but in the short term, resentment can be pretty damn useful for growth.

After my divorce, resentment was a blessing in disguise for my future love life. While I was in my marriage, I was focused mainly on what I could do to fix it. I felt it was all up to me to get it sorted. That was bullshit. And it's so obvious now! The anger and resentment that came later didn't linger, but they did teach me some important lessons. Including: *I am good enough, it's okay to be different, and I deserve kindness.* Those lessons sent me off into the dating world knowing my value and what I won't tolerate again. It took some time, persistence, and lots of first dates (perhaps I'll save those horror stories for another book), but I refused to settle and eventually, I found the love of my life. He treats me like a queen and likes all the same parts of me that I think are cool, which is so important, and something I'd never experienced before. If I hadn't gone through that sea of resentment, I wouldn't have grown up enough to attract such an amazing guy and recognize him as such.

Resentment came to my aid again later, this time at work. My second to last full-time healthcare job was for a hospice agency where I had a boss who wound up being key to jumpstarting my career transition. In my job there I was being openly and publicly bullied by the medical director (male) in a way that completely undermined my authority on the team. The boss shined me on, validated my complaints, but was in no hurry to change the status quo. Following multiple public attacks on my character (of which this boss and the entire agency were aware), I flat out refused to work with the medical director anymore. This infuriated the boss, but I persisted, went over her head and won: medical director was fired, I was vindicated. However, the working relationship I had with my boss was never the same after that.

I knew she was trying to get rid of me months later when she rescinded vacation time she'd long since previously approved. I already had plans all made and airline tickets bought to take my kids to visit my mom at that point so this was a problem. As a compromise, I offered to work remotely (which was totally doable to meet the needs of the job) during my vacation. She declined. Then I offered to change to per diem status (worse for me financially, but I was motivated to keep my job) so the time off could be unpaid. She refused that, too. It had become a one-way street (*her* way) and I didn't like where it was going. So in April of 2019, I quit, on principle.

In retrospect, her awfulness helped me move on and explore a new direction, new possibilities I probably wouldn't have pursued if it had been a more comfortable situation. She sparked my sense of injustice and I responded by doubling down. I strengthened my faith in myself and my value as important and worthy of respect, peace and fulfillment. Just like everyone else in my life who I encourage to seek these things for themselves, I knew my time had come. She forced me out of the nest of healthcare. And I really needed that push.

What I gained from my resentment was accelerated growth. I knew I needed to leave healthcare, but I was deeply risk adverse. I'm not sure how long it would've taken me to make any significant changes if this hadn't happened. This situation left me no choice but to figure out another way of living with less suckage of my soul. And I *did* figure it out.

I resisted a new choking leash of full-time employment, bought my own damn health insurance, and found some smaller healthcare gigs to sustain me financially. I basically built a freelance career in which I could retain control of my time in an industry that doesn't traditionally support that type of arrangement. This freedom gave me a new lease on life. I finally felt like I was in charge, and that my time was not beholden to any single employer. Losing the weight of that burden freed up brain space for my creativity to return. I started writing *a ton*. About all kinds of crap—cooking, recipes, philosophy, dive bars, dating. You name it and I was writing about it. The creative storm was unleashed! And now, I'm still steadily making my way completely out of healthcare. Once again—thank you, resentment! I owe you one.

Life is too short to be miserable.

Regret

Regret: *feeling sad, repentant, or disappointed over something that has happened or been done, especially a loss or missed opportunity*

"When you get older, it's not about what you did that you regret, it's what you didn't do."

—Grace Slick, American singer and musician

It's 3 a.m. I'm wide awake, and regret is keeping me company.

This is one of the emotions I have the most trouble making peace with and accepting as part of the process of falling out of love. It feels ugly and shameful. And, it would seem, inevitable.

Thankfully, it's usually fleeting. For me, it's often about leaving a job and (perceived) financial security. My internal dialogue goes something like this: *Was I crazy to leave that job that gave me health insurance, a 401k, and a big, juicy, reliable salary? It wasn't that bad.* But it also goes something like this: *You were fucking miserable, remember?*

The hard part is taking myself on my word about the latter. Was I really *that* miserable? Couldn't I have just stuck it out, done the minimum, and continued to collect that steady pay-check?

Now that I've had some time and distance to recover from full-time work in healthcare, the answer sometimes seems like maybe I could have (or even should have) stayed. And that doubt and regret feel heavy. I felt it when I was leaving my marriage, too. All that second guessing myself, not wanting it to be a total loss, chucking aside all that time and shared history together. It felt wrong to just "give up".

There's no way to sugarcoat it. Life transformation is not easy, and there are no guarantees.

Remembering my earlier experience falling out of love when I divorced my husband is comforting when I have regretful feelings about leaving my career. More time has passed since my marriage broke up in which I've gained a truer perspective, and this is helpful and, hopefully, a glimpse of my future connection with my present career choices. I felt doubt and regret after separating from my husband. I felt like a failure, like I was thrashing about and making a mess of my life. Now, seven years later as I write this, I can see that it was absolutely the right decision. My marriage really *was* that bad. My regrets about my divorce have lost their teeth; now they are mild, blessedly brief, and more of the variety of regretting I stayed so long! I recognize now that regret happens because I cared so much about my marriage and about my career. Those feelings run deep, even when they eventually run their course. I'm banking on this being true for this massive career change as well.

Ultimately, I believe I will at least have less regret trying for a better fit in my career as opposed to not trying and simply sticking with what is familiar but no longer fulfilling.

I try to hold regret loosely. I acknowledge that it comes and goes, and that it's important, but I also take comfort that it is likely to be a temporary feeling. I don't let it permanently derail me and send me spinning backwards.

I don't regret my first career or my first marriage. I was a different person when I started both. Good things came out of both of those chapters in the book of my life. My marriage included a lot of fun and laughter (before it turned to tears) and produced two amazing kids. My career allowed me to gain expertise and satisfaction in helping people through difficult things. I feel proud of the work I did in healthcare. Time and experience have reshaped me, though. Neither my career nor my first marriage fits who I am today. And neither warrants lifelong regret.

Regret today dishonors the choices I made way back then, and they weren't all bad decisions. Things have changed, I have changed, those days are over, and it's time to turn the page to the next chapter.

Life is too short to be miserable.

Dissonance

Dissonance: *a tension or clash resulting from the combination of two disharmonious or unsuitable elements*

"Dissonance (if you are interested) leads to discovery."

—William Carlos Williams, American poet

The dissonance I felt as a healthcare worker was a key factor in my decision to make a big change and pursue a more creative life. My mental distress was confusing, because I'd played by all the rules. I went to college, achieved a respectable career, trundled off to work every day determined to do good, yet couldn't figure out why I persistently felt low-key dissatisfied. And even downright miserable at times. It was clear that something was amiss. My internal experience of my external reality was off—*way* off. I spent much time vacillating between feeling like there's something better for me out there and try-ing desperately to feel good in my life, to be grateful for what I have and all that I've been given. My then-spouse uncharitably explained my feelings away as just more examples of how selfish, ungrateful, and impossible to satisfy I am. Of course, *that* actually *was* an effective way to trick me into compliance, to get me to conform in order to prove him wrong. What a silly girl I was to take that bait.

But am I selfish, or is it more accurate to say I'm self-affirming?

Trying to overcome my people pleasing ways is hard. I want to be the good girl who behaves as expected, yet another part of me wants to break free and express my true, inner being. Gloriously, deliciously, colorfully, boldly, bawdily. But how to reconcile this with the values handed down to me from my parents and my culture about the importance of being a hard worker, when what I really want is freedom and time to create, time to enjoy my life? With all this recently acquired newfound freedom on my hands, I've struggled with feeling like I'm not putting in enough time. *I'm not as busy as everyone else and, therefore, I'm not a hard worker. I must be lazy.*

But I *am* productive. I've written 25,000 words on this book so far (edit: no surprise to you at this point, but I did eventually finish it), in addition to various and sundry articles, recipes, and dive bar reviews. All of this while still managing the rest of my life responsibilities and relationships. I am obviously not lazy. But I am far from busy. There's a difference.

Can you be busy and *not* productive? Yes.

Can you be productive and *not* busy? Also yes.

So what constitutes a hard worker? Is it busyness or is it productivity?

My head says it's productivity that matters. What you actually "make", despite how much or how little time you spend on it. Take writing for instance. I spend a lot of time thinking about what I'm going to write. Some of it is conscious, but a lot (if not most) of it is boiling and bubbling there under the surface as I go about my life. While I may appear to be lazing on the couch watching TV, cooking in my kitchen, reading a book, driving around or walking my dog, I'm actually working in my head on coherent thoughts to later put down on paper. The time I spend actively writing? Maybe a couple of hours per day—on a good day. The quality of what I actually produce is what matters to me. And a lot goes into that: experience, education, daydreaming, reading, contemplation, rest, bad TV.

However, I know that busyness makes me *look like* I'm working hard. Hard workers are busy workers. They toil away at their desks to all hours, always appear harried, stressed and stretched almost to the breaking point. This is what my culture expects from its worker bees. Under this system of thought, I can actually be productive and still be perceived as a lazy loser. Or I can choose being busy and overscheduled with meaningless bullshit, often at the expense of my own wellbeing and be praised for being such a hard worker—regardless of what I do or do not produce. Still with me?

This is fucked up.

Being busy does not necessarily make you productive, nor does it make you a hard worker. It just makes you busy. And possibly miserable in your life, because you don't have enough time for what really matters. At least that's how it was for me. Busyness is actually wasting energy, not working hard. It is poorly managing a limited resource: time. In my opinion, this is not a sign of a hard worker but of an *ignorant* worker, and someone who will likely be praised for being "such a hard worker". This kind of shit makes my head want to explode.

Yet, I *still* have guilt about not working "hard" enough, which is really just me feeling self-conscious that I'm not as busy as everyone else. *Sigh.*

Life is too short to be miserable.

Pride

Pride: *a feeling of deep pleasure or satisfaction derived from one's own achievements, the achievements of those with whom one is closely associated, or from qualities or possessions that are widely admired*

"Disciplining yourself to do what you know is right and important, although difficult, is the high road to pride, self-esteem, and personal satisfaction."

—Margaret Thatcher, former Prime Minister of the United Kingdom

I don't feel pride in my healthcare career anymore. I'm just going through the motions. Lifeless. A place holder, like the person who's hired to sit in some celebrity's seat while they get up to go pee during awards shows.

I do feel pride in other parts of my life. I have raised two wonderful, healthy, and well-adjusted kids. I am one half of a flourishing romantic partnership. I have "cuted-up" my house and garden. I am a good daughter and sister and friend. I think (and hope) that I bring joy to people in my life, and I am proud of this. This is good stuff.

Part of my malaise at work is my own fault. I have effectively disconnected myself from opportunities for meaningful work in healthcare. I have backed away from the heavy lifting of daily clinical care out of self-preservation. I am learning that an unfortunate consequence of fading into the background like this is that there are fewer opportunities to feel proud of my work. I do feel good about how I treat patients, and I try to be a welcome, caring presence. I think that has value. And educating the next generation of hospice nurses *definitely* has value. But neither of these things really makes me feel great about my work. Just so-so, like I'm biding my time.

I wanted this distance though. I made it happen because, deep in my heart, I know these present roles are the stepping stones toward the kind of work that really lights me up. And you know what? I'm pretty proud of myself for taking this leap. For facing my fears, going against the norm, leaving the well-worn expected path and making a big change. I want to dive in and write about anything and everything. I have a lot stored up that I want to say. I want to write about relationships, family values, menopause, parenting teenagers and adult children, more dive bars and recipes and travel. So many fun topics to explore! Sometimes I dream about how I'll feel once I am a published author, and this reminds me what pride in my work feels like. I feel pride in just getting myself going in a new direction, too. That's no small feat.

Life is too short to be miserable.

Hope

Hope: *a feeling of expectation and desire for a certain thing to happen*

"Hope is a passion for the possible."

—Søren Kierkegaard, Danish philosopher

Without hope, I would have never undertaken this crazy journey. In the depths of my despair about working in healthcare, a quiet knowing, deep inside, persisted:

There is something better for me out there.

I don't think I would have gotten divorced or left healthcare if I didn't believe that on some level. Even just a teeny bit. What would be the point?

Without hope there is just resignation. Plod along, be grateful for what you have, don't make a fuss, don't raise your head above the roofline. Don't rock the boat or upset the apple cart. I am absolutely awed by how such tiny phrases like these are deviously designed and effective in keeping us towing the line of conformity. Fuck that noise.

Hope brings the juice. It is a belief in the future having the potential to be better than the present or the past.

Hope is the motivation behind resilience. It is what helps us to resist giving up on ourselves and settling in to just accept our lot in life. No matter what bad stuff has happened, hope persists. It keeps our hearts open when circumstances push us to pull inside ourselves and form a tight little protective ball. Hope says, "Go ahead and have a rest and lick your wounds, but then we are moving the fuck on, because there is good stuff ahead."

My life at work and in my marriage was miserable. On the outside, all looked fine. But on the inside, I was terribly unfulfilled. And sad. Hope was the (dim) light of a better future in which I could be alive and vibrant instead of just enduring and staying the course. Hope triumphed when I left my marriage, and my love life blossomed into everything I had ever dreamed of. So why not expect an equally good result with leaving my healthcare career? Wow, this chapter is really getting cheesy. But a certain amount of figurative cheese is almost unavoidable when talking about hope, because it *is* kind of spiritual. Deal with it.

Life is too short to be miserable.

Recap

That was a taste of some of the shit I went through that helped cement the idea in my head that, well, life is too short to be miserable. Even when in the midst of making a change for the better, misery always seems to come along for the ride in the form of denial, despair, and so on and so on. But this misery is different. It is not interminable misery; it is *constructive* misery. It is instructive and it drew my attention to where I needed to grow and what needed to be fixed.

Life is too short to be miserable.

Part 2: Handle Your Shit

Stabilize the Ship

Before I could totally own that I was terminally miserable in my healthcare career and in my marriage, I tried to save both. I worked for a couple of different hospices, thinking that a change of scene might bring back my passion for the work. It didn't. Neither did counseling or moving back to Washington save my marriage. Both were doomed, the marriage just fell apart first.

Two years after my dad and brother died, I found myself a newly single mom living in a new state with only a limited social support system in place. I felt an overwhelming, primal need to stabilize the ship beneath my little family—emotionally, physically, and financially. I resolved to reinvent my family life in order to grow happy, healthy kids. Without a daily dad presence. This didn't afford much opportunity or brain space to question my own destiny and what made me content and happy. For a period of time, it was all about survival. Handling my shit.

Once I got my feet back under me though, I couldn't ignore how much I felt less and less interested and engaged in my work. Health insurance companies made practicing conscientiously more and more difficult, if not impossible. Patients seemed increasingly needy, and were often pugnaciously prickly consumers. I tried new jobs, new niches within healthcare—even teaching—but, ultimately, I couldn't ignore how miserable I was at my core. I just didn't want to be immersed in this sea of sickness and death and misery anymore. I didn't want to work so hard trying to provide good or even adequate care for people within a broken system. I didn't want to fight the establishment (even though it might be a good fight); I just wanted out. Every inch of my being was crying out for change. Even my brain was resisting; I had zero capacity for new learning which was unfamiliar and really upsetting. Even long held information that should have been deeply ingrained in my brain started completely falling out of my head. Very inconvenient, and very impossible to ignore. I had to figure this out, because, as we've hopefully established by now, life is too short to be miserable. I needed some action, some movement in a better—or at least new—direction. This movement led to many uncomfortable emotions. Emotions that made it obvious that I really needed to handle my shit on this score or risk staying miserable *forever*.

Handle your shit.

Duty

Duty: *a moral or legal obligation; a responsibility*

"When work is a pleasure, life is a joy! When work is a duty, life is slavery."

—Maxim Gorky, Russian author

It's easy to wield duty as a weapon, usually to incite guilt or shame in another (or in oneself). To get them to comply with what is expected, which is sometimes also what is "right". But not always.

The American healthcare system is unmatched in using duty to control its workforce. Many well-intentioned people, myself included, enter healthcare careers as a means to live out our altruistic inclinations. Corporations within the healthcare system are only too happy to use this sense of duty we have toward our patients to keep us working in deplorable conditions. Burned out, beholden to insurance companies, overscheduled, underappreciated, and expected to sacrifice the wellbeing of our families and ourselves in order to serve "the cause". If we squawk, it just proves how we aren't *really* dedicated. If we were, we would abide by our moral duty to serve without question or complaint. What bullshit. But it *is* very effective in keeping us quiet and chained to our jobs, even when those jobs start to impact our health and sanity.

But that's not even the aspect of duty I really want to discuss here. There's a different, even darker side of duty masquerading as noble and self-sacrificing. It's when I use duty as an excuse to get out of doing hard things. My much needed and desired career shift has been put on the back burner for probably the past ten years for all sorts of "good" reasons. My duties to be responsible financially, to raise my kids, to be a loving spouse, to care for my aging mom, to maintain my friendships, and to have a meaningful career in which I selflessly make a difference in people's lives. These concerns take precedence, and they leave me no time to pursue my own happiness and fulfillment.

These are excuses. My excuses. Things I tell myself to morally justify staying stuck in the status quo of my dead-end career. Doesn't matter if they're all duties that are morally beyond reproach; I'm still using them to keep myself down. I'm telling myself, lying to myself really, that my needs are less important than literally everything else and everyone else in my life. That I have a duty to everyone else except myself. Does that sound healthy? To accept remaining miserable in my career, just like I did for years in my marriage? I think it is pathetic and unnecessary. Marriage *can* and *should* be a joy. Same with work. And I will make room in my life for that joy. For *my* joy.

Handle your shit.

Fear

Fear: an unpleasant emotion caused by the belief that someone or something is dangerous, likely to cause pain or a threat

"Ultimately, we know deeply that the other side of every fear is freedom."

—Marilyn Ferguson, American author

I've had lots of fears during this process. Fear of change. Fear of fucking up. Fear of financial ruin. Fear of ridicule. Fear of failure and having to go back to work in healthcare, with my tail tucked between my legs and endure the disproving looks from my former colleagues. Fear of judgment, from everyone. Fear that, at some point, I will have to explain this big gap in my resume and my checkered work history for the last several years. Fear of success. Fear of the unknown. So much fucking fear! It aggravates my anxiety and paralyzes my process. Fear was holding me back from growth. From taking needed risks. This fear situation needed management, ASAP, if I was ever going to get anywhere. Or at least anywhere good.

Ignoring it was futile—it just showed up in my dreams or in other guises (anxiety) to torment me. Ballsy courage helped me get moving toward a new career, but fear was hanging on for the ride with its hands covering my eyes. This was incredibly unpleasant. At some point, I recognized that if I couldn't eliminate fear, at least I could try to change my relationship with it.

I worked on retraining my brain to instead see fear as evidence of moving in the right direction, even if I didn't feel it in my heart right away. I just kept telling myself, "Fear is forward motion." It took time for my mind to adapt to this suggestion, and I still feel overwhelmed by fear at times, but the difference is that now it no longer feels totally disabling. I've come to understand that, like all emotions, fear too will pass.

It also helps that my feelings of fear related to taking my career in a totally different direction have slowly given way to its sister emotion: excitement. Just brief glimpses at first, wee peeks of what could be, but it keeps me moving forward, fear or no fear.

I also try not to look too far ahead and freak myself out. I just focus on taking concrete steps, one after another, doable steps in the right direction—or at least in a new one. Even without certainty.

Fear isn't all bad. Some fear can be useful. It serves a purpose, and we need it. The healthy kind keeps us from falling off of tall buildings, eating unidentified mushrooms, having unprotected sex, or gambling away our IRA. The unhealthy kind, however, the kind that holds us back from achieving our dreams—yeah, that one needs to loosen its grip.

Handle your shit.

Grief and Loss

Grief: *deep sorrow, especially that caused by someone's death*

Loss: *the state of feeling of grief when deprived of someone or something of value*

"Grieving is like going to the bathroom. If you try to hold it in, bad things happen." —Steven Shomler, American author

"Loss is a part of life. If you don't have loss, you don't grow." —Dominick Cruz, American mixed martial artist

I've had my share of losses throughout this process of leaving my old career. Some I expected. Others were surprising. Here's a bunch of them:

Loss of comfort zone. It's nice to know what you're going to be doing every day and what is expected of you without having to think about it too hard.

Loss of feeling like an expert. It was pleasant to be able to solve problems quickly and effectively. And to be appreciated by others for this ability.

Loss of respect. Loved ones are puzzled why I'm taking such risks at this point in my life when I "should" be coasting toward retirement.

Loss of identity. Healthcare, especially hospice, is a noble profession. When I told people what I did for a living, they would invariably respond with something akin to, "Awww, that must be so hard. You are an angel!" Having that immediate validation from strangers was pretty sweet.

Loss of shared identity with others about the trials and tribulations associated with "working for the man". I don't relate much anymore to complaints about bad bosses, horrible commutes, and the general angst that comes with reluctantly working in an unfulfilling career in a royally fucked-up industry. Those are just blessedly distant, bad memories for me.

Loss of income. I liked making big money. I liked having health insurance paid for by my employer. It's definitely not cheap on the open market! I liked getting automatic paycheck deposits every two weeks with my retirement savings and taxes already taken out.

Loss of a future. I'm upgrading to a new and better future, but, still, loss of the old one is a loss all the same. Just as when my marriage died—loss of the vision of that particular future has an impact. What could have been. Old hopes and dreams.

I believe grieving, in the context of career change, is a means to move past these losses while acknowledging their importance. It's about learning to let go of old relationships, old identities, and old ways of doing and being. Deep down, I know that this career path is no longer meant for me, but it is incredibly hard to let go of it completely. So much of myself and my history is wrapped up in it. It is old, dead wood, but still—I'm losing a part of me.

Not everything is a painful loss, though. I will *gladly* let go of my healthcare knowledge. Flush away those files and make room for more song lyrics! Renewing my licenses? Definitely won't miss that. So expensive, and so many annoying bureaucratic hoops. Worrying about getting enough continuing education hours each year—I will eagerly give that up, too. No longer having to be the one with all the answers will be a relief. Being part of a shitty healthcare system that is broken beyond repair? That's an easy goodbye.

But. This is all I have ever known in my adult life. Even though it's liberating in some ways to start over, there's everything that gets left behind, too. Learning from the losses of my dad and brother and my first marriage, I know how important it is to take the time to recognize and grieve *all* losses, especially the big ones. It is part of the process of letting go and moving forward. Trying to skip grieving will just see it come out sideways—perhaps as unhealthy coping behaviors (too much booze or other numbing strategies), poor concentration, anger, anxiety, depression, or bad decisions. Pick your poison. It doesn't just go away, though, without active participation.

To effectively grieve, you've got to pay attention to whatever is painfully absent and let it run its course. The depth of the loss will influence the length and depth of the grief experienced. I've talked about how hard I grieved after I lost my dad and brother. Oceans of tears. And they didn't only come out when I wanted them to, neatly at a scheduled time. Nope! Seeing Father's Day cards in the store and realizing I would never ever buy one again for sure set off a flood of tears. Celebrating my brother Mike's birthday, ten days after his death was a trigger. Attending the memorial service that Mike had helped plan for dad, a service that ended up morphing into a joint celebration for both of them, was devastating. He planned his own memorial service...how unbelievably tragic. And, sometimes, just certain songs would come on and surprise me with a tidal wave of grief. It was a disorienting time in which I felt outside of my body, just hanging on for the ride, pummeled from every direction by an unseen force greater than anything I had ever known.

It makes sense, though. These were two of the most important people in my life, so it took a while to process the magnitude of my loss. After that year of dedicated grieving, it eased up, but didn't completely go away. I still have wavelets of grief for them from time to time. Many while writing this book, in fact. I like to think they would be proud of me. What's different now is that I enjoy getting these waves. It *is* painful, but it's also nice to remember them and how much I loved them.

Grieving my marriage was a different experience, but no less important. My feelings about my former husband and our time together were complicated. So too was my grieving process. Compared to Mike and dad, it felt less clean, less linear. Honestly, I felt much more angry and disappointed. But it has still been healing to review it all, feel it all, learn from it all and let it go.

The grief I am feeling about my career feels very similar to the end of my marriage in its complexity. Healthcare was an important chapter of my life and as such earns my respect, and I will grieve it appropriately. Even though I'm leaving my career voluntarily same as I did my marriage, it still hurts to say goodbye forever. A combination of walking and then journaling helps me a lot with this type of internal process-ing. Making time for movement gets my thoughts a-churning. Putting down my uncensored words in print helps get them out of my head (and heart). I do these things daily to help myself get through it. The world doesn't stop for grief though, so I will (attempt to) compartmentalize the processing of this loss while I keep moving on to better things.

Handle your shit.

Discouragement

Discouragement: *having less confidence or enthusiasm*

"The most essential factor is persistence—the determination never to allow your energy or enthusiasm to be dampened by the discouragement that must inevitably come."

—James Whitcomb Riley, American author

I selected the above quote for this section because I think it is complete BULLSHIT! Well, maybe not *complete* bullshit, but bullshitty for sure (sorry James Whitcomb Riley). The parts about discouragement being inevitable and persistence being vital are true, but the bit about keeping your energy and enthusiasm up all the time is what makes me angry. This is such an unhelpful denial of normal feelings.

I know, at least in my journey, discouragement has been a frequent, unwelcome visitor. Like a bad penny, this one keeps popping up and giving me fits. It is a voice that persistently tells me that work will always be hard and unpleasant. *I'll never make it as a writer, and my stuff is shit. How could this ever work out?* Dark days at times.

I call this voice Dour Dan. Giving him a name makes him human and thus easier to understand and manage. Is it weird to personify emotions? Maybe so, but I think it helps. *Oh, that's just Dan, coming around again under his perpetual cloud.* I say hi and he eventually moves on, taking his cloud with him.

But Dan is right—about some things. I don't have any guarantees of success in my new venture. and there is no view of a clear path forward. I also accept that I can't go backward either, because I was miserable there. So here I am, trapped in the middle between one closed door and endless horizon ahead. And it's difficult at times not to feel depressed and discouraged about that.

Rather than ignore or numb out or try to steamroll these genuine feelings with false positivity, I try to be gentle with them. I give myself permission to sit with these difficult emotions instead of rushing to action in an effort to banish them or trying to candy coat them into submission by looking for the "bright side". Embracing the ugliness of feeling discouraged, I've found, is a more helpful way forward. It is a true representation of my internal world; it is part of me. And it is there because I am stretching myself, trying to grow in a new direction. This is important to me, or else I wouldn't care so much about failing. I think of difficult emotions like this as people that just want their voices to be heard, and then once they are seen, they are satisfied for the moment and get out of the way. And then I can move on and keep growing and going forward.

Handle your shit.

Faith

Faith: *complete trust or confidence in someone or something*

"Faith is taking the first step, even when you don't see the whole staircase."

—Martin Luther King Jr., American minister and activist

Faith that there is greener grass elsewhere.

Faith to reject the status quo without proof that something better exists.

Faith in myself to "make it" as a writer.

Faith that the words will come.

Faith in the universe to guide me and that it will all work out, even if I can't imagine how.

Faith is fucking scary! Especially for a planner like me. I want to stand on my tiptoes and try to see over the wall to judge if going over is a good idea. Faith says, "Sorry, buddy—gotta pay the price of admission and go in blind. But it's good on the other side. I promise", with a *wink wink.*

Faith is the active expression of hope. It was faith that kept me going in order to survive—deaths, divorce, unemployment, moving on without a job lined up. Faith was remaining engaged with life, even when I felt riddled with doubt. I just kept going anyway. Hope helped me to believe that better times would return after the darkness, and faith was the engine that kept me moving. These experiences have increased my resilience. I can handle hard shit; I've proven it. Reflecting on these things makes me feels stronger, bolder.

Nevertheless, I'm struggling with faith right now. I feel like the universe is nudging me to let go of healthcare work completely, and I am scared to do it. An apropos analogy here is when I finally left my marriage. I didn't know how it was going to work out, but I did it anyway because I had faith in myself and hope that a better life existed for me. It was a really weak and beat up faith at that time, but it was there. I know it's time to bring her out again and dust her off for service, but I am scared. This feels almost like a bigger leap than when I left my marriage. Maybe because back then, I was still in the fog of mourning my dad and brother when I divorced; everything was hazy anyway, so adding divorce to the mix of misery didn't move the freak-out needle too much.

Letting go of one thing to make room for something better requires leaning heavily on faith. There is strong evidence it has worked out for me in the past, and those reflections are empowering. Story time: I have a weird predilection for the number 4. It feels powerful, meaningful, and prophetic for me. It's my favoritest, luckiest number. I'm not weirdly superstitious; just a healthy, quirky amount. It's fun! So when I turned 44, I changed a bunch of my passwords to something akin to 44isthegreatestyear as a sort of affirmation of all the wonderful things that I was certain would be coming to me that year. So—what cool things happened that year? I got divorced. Yep. Definitely didn't feel much like the greatest year at the time! Felt more like a cruel joke. With time and distance though (and this is going to sound annoyingly cute and sappy, but it is true), I did and do see my divorce and the new start it gave me as a wonderful gift. Separating from my husband was necessary pain to make way for a better fitting life. And love. I'm skipping over a lot of important stuff here, but my new husband appeared a few years later and I am happier in my love life than I ever imagined I could be.

In retrospect, 44 was indeed a very good year and put me on a much better trajectory. I knew it! Naysayers of superstition be damned!

Maybe this is what holds me back at times from making big leaps in my career, though—the other parts of my life, non-career stuff, are really good right now and I don't want to fuck them up! I have a great husband and I'm enjoying being in a relationship more than I ever have before in my life. My kids are happy, healthy, and all headed in good directions. They are smart and grounded, so I don't need to do a lot of active parenting, just some guidance and lots of love (and cooking—the teenagers still at home sure can eat!). I have a cute, peaceful home (we call it HavenHome, sorry for the sappiness). My mortgage is my only debt. I have lots of available credit and some money in the bank, as well as some set aside for the kids' college funds and retirement. I'm physically healthy and I continue to grow emotionally. Do I really want to potentially upset the entire apple cart for work satisfaction? Am I being greedy for "wanting it all"? Is it even possible to have all aspects of your life rocking at the same time? Is this like when you bypass that perfectly good parking spot, thinking you can get one a little bit closer and then being shut out and relegated to the back forty?

Sometimes I feel like other people's faith in me is stronger than my own. My husband is my biggest cheerleader and seems to have unfailing faith in my skill as a writer. As I am writing this, I worry about failing him. What if I'm not as good as he thinks? What if his faith in me has been misplaced? What if he thinks my stuff is good only because he's blinded by his love for me? Well, there's only one way to find out, so I'll press on and keep writing this pap, remembering those past leaps that worked out and bolstering my faith that wherever this exercise leads me, it will be worthwhile.

My intellectual mind understands the wisdom of this. My heart needs to catch up.

Handle your shit.

Resilience

Resilience: *the process of adapting well in the face of adversity, trauma, tragedy, threats or significant sources of stress*

"Of course fear does not automatically lead to courage. Injury does not necessarily lead to insight. Hardship will not automatically make us better. Pain can break us or make us wiser. Suffering can destroy us or make us stronger. Fear can cripple us, or it can make us more courageous. It is resilience that makes the difference."

—Eric Greitens, American former politician

Resilience, to me, is about choosing to handle the shitty stuff that comes my way like a boss. I've come to understand that life sends each of us a series of unique challenges, and it is up to us to become either bitter or better as a result. The choice is ours. The choice always is.

Wallowing in self-pity might be an unavoidable and necessary short-term indulgence when the shit hits the fan. An indulgence best shared with friends. And wine. It can also become a trap, if not careful. I refuse to assume the identity of a victim. I may have been victimized at times in my life, but that is *not* who I am. Victimhood that persists and becomes permanent is incredibly tiresome, not to mention a waste of time and effort. It's hard to move forward if you stay stuck lamenting the past.

We all have bad stuff happen. And it is not a competition to see who has it worse. But we do have choices about how we make sense of our personal trials and tragedies. I'm not suggesting here that we should just stoically bear it and move on. Quite the opposite, in fact. I believe it is vitally important that we make time to learn from our misfortunes. The alternative is to risk continuing to bring the same shit upon ourselves, over and over again, consciously or unconsciously.

For instance, many dating people tell themselves they are single against their will due to external factors beyond their control such as a global lack of suitable partners. Or that they keep getting into bad relationships because they themselves are hopelessly flawed as humans and their "picker is broken" (I have actually heard this, in real life). Well, is that really true that there is nobody good out there, or could self-reflection uncover some shit you need to deal with, deep inside, that leads you to remain single? Or maybe you've kept moving from relationship to relationship, in constant motion like a shark who'll die if it stops swimming, never taking any time alone to reflect on what you could learn from what went wrong? An examination of past failures might offer insight as to why you continue to unconsciously make bad picks. Go ahead, take a look. It can't hurt (much).

I realize not everything bad that happens in life may be attributed to our own unconscious resistance to responsibility and growth. There is plenty that happens to us truly through no apparent fault of our own. Wrong place, wrong time, and all that. But, even in those situations, you have to deal with the fallout anyway, and there's likely still some useful stuff to learn.

An example from my own journey involves shit that went down when I was a kid. I know I was loved, but I was also put in harm's way on multiple occasions. I'm sure my parents believed I was in good enough hands, but I wasn't. And bad things happened to me that could have been avoided. Many more might have occurred but were thankfully near-misses (my inner parent looks back now and kind of cringes in disbelief). I know my un-examined feelings about those unfortunate events tormented me and likely influenced some risky behavior on my part in my younger years. Not proud of that, but I was trying to move on and just gloss over it all, telling myself I was *fine*. In retrospect, that was a mistake. I was *not* fine. I kept it together, but I was not ok. My parents were responsible for putting me in those situations, but I've never blamed them for what went down way back then. It was the 70s, kids were raised free-range, they were doing their best. I don't need or want anything from them to heal. That's up to me. And I'm not writing about this now as a way to publicly shame them. What parents out there *haven't* made mistakes? All I'm saying is that I endured some shit in my childhood that was not good, but I survived. I did my work to heal. And I'm kind to myself whenever difficult thoughts and feelings well up about what I experienced instead of immediately pushing them away. Most importantly, though, is how this has positively influenced my own parenting. No way in hell was I going to make those same mistakes with my precious babes. I'm sure I've made and will continue to make others, but not those! This experience also helped me learn the tough but vital lesson that bad stuff needs to be processed before I can successfully move beyond it.

Whenever I'm trying to make sense of crap that comes my way, by fate or by my own stupid choices, I choose to sit with my yuck with an open heart and mind. Turn it over in my brain, and examine it from different angles in the light. Feel it. See what it has to teach me, about myself, others, the world.

Good or bad. Sometimes I gain insight into other people, our culture, beliefs and institutions. These help me to do a better job of navigating life in the future, and not just merely existing and letting myself be blown in all directions by the prevailing winds.

I don't always like what I find in myself, to be sure. Like the fact that I married my first husband even though I knew on some level it wasn't right. Or that I jumped into a career in healthcare that I maybe could have seen didn't really fit who I was as a person if I had taken things slower. In both cases, impetuosity got me into trouble. But I was so goddamned eager to be done with school, settled in my career and snugly married with a family. The immediacy of *done now* (marriage, career choice) at the expense of *done right*. Ugly, but true. Embarrassing to own, but true. However, there is a reward for this pain: I learned from both experiences how to more effectively tune into my internal wisdom and take my time, especially on big, life changing decisions like these. There is no room for ego in this exercise of learning from our mistakes.

I refuse to let this—or any other bad stuff—own my ass though. Whether I come by my challenges through my own bad decisions or sheer, dumb luck, I will keep growing as a result. I will make my troubles work for me. This is what I mean by resilience. And I am challenging myself right now by taking these career and financial risks. Will it work out? I hope so, but I don't know for sure if it will. What I *am* sure of is that I have handled difficult things before, and if I fail on this, I will survive. And I'll likely be better for it.

Handle your shit.

Persistence

Persistence: *continuing firmly or obstinately in a course of action in spite of difficulty or opposition*

"Paralyze resistance with persistence."

—Woody Hayes, American football player

The last thing I feel this morning is persistent.

I woke up feeling discouraged, feeling like everything I'm doing with my life and everything I've written is shit.

I got my computer out, all set to write, and then proceeded to fall into my phone for an hour and a half. It's amazing how many interesting tunnels you can find in Instagram or TikTok when you're avoiding writing.

But writers write.

And I am a writer.

Persistence is not always a virtue, though. There is benefit in knowing when to quit and adjust course. Staying in my first marriage or my first career would have been foolish. Persisting in pursing my writer dreams is wise. I hope.

But wisdom is knowing the difference.

I am sure that I am a writer, and I must persist.

So I opened up this damn computer and here we are.

At risk of sounding schmaltzy, I must report that some of my best stuff is written on days like these, on which I've had seemingly insurmountable inertia at the start. Go figure.

Handle your shit.

Desperation

Desperation: *a loss of hope or a great need that can make you act irrationally*

Many of the quotes I came across for desperation were about how it is a necessary part of creativity and how it spurs action. A motivating force. I think that is a crock of shit. For me, I believe desperation is a vital element—in making bad decisions. So, I guess I'll just go ahead and quote myself here, dammit.

"Desperation leads to bad decisions."

—KC Shomler, American bestselling author

Oh, just let me revel in it a bit, won't you?

Ahem. Moving on...

Back to the brilliant (ok, maybe not brilliant, but certainly accurate) quote of mine: whilst tiptoeing away from full-time healthcare employment, I would have intermittent financial freakouts of varying degrees. Sometimes minor, and sometimes full-blown panic attacks about how if I didn't go back into full-time employment immediately, we would surely wind up penniless and living on the street. I knew deep down this was desperation talking, but without the benefit of a clear vision forward it felt crazy and irresponsible *not* to take another job.

I remember when I quit full-time employment in healthcare (the first time), due to the ethical divide that resulted in a stalemate with that awful former boss, I felt good about the reasons why I quit. Unfortunately, I was also horribly desperate to find a new job, immediately. This is part of what we are taught right? *Don't quit a job without something else lined up and don't have any gaps in your resume.* Christ on a crutch—I failed on both.

So I set about to get me some job offers (gratefully, it's really not that hard to do in healthcare), singled out the best prospect, and negotiated myself a sweet deal. My issue was that as the start date approached, I felt increasingly physically ill and emotionally distraught. Seriously, my body and brain were in full-on rebellion mode. It was freaky. It was like a force inside me rising up and refusing to allow me to torture myself anymore. There was no way around it. I closed my eyes, held my breath, and cancelled my start date. Turned down a perfectly good job just like that. Was I fucking crazy? Little bit, yep.

And then the money panic set in.

And it led me to a slew of bad decisions. Out of desperation, I applied for—and got—a whole bunch of healthcare jobs I didn't want. Some I took and regretted later. Some I took and slogged through until I just couldn't stand the misery anymore. I felt physically ill and deeply heartsick at the prospect of continuing to do that kind of work. Healthcare used to bring me joy until it started to feel like a mean bully giving me regular beatdowns in the schoolyard. But my fear of financial ruin was equally strong so I kept taking those jobs. At one point I think I had 3 or 4 part-time jobs at once. It sounds crazy and it was crazy, but I was desperate for some semblance of financial security.

In the summer of 2020 the world was in the midst of a global pandemic, vaccines were still a ways off and life for me and many people felt deeply unsettled. I was just over a year into my forced exodus from full-time employment and feeling far from stable financially. Right on cue, a cushy job in healthcare landed in my lap. It was full-time but "easy" and would allow me to make some "easy" money without scraping by at multiple jobs. I told myself this would allow me to focus more on writing. I think I knew it was a bad idea at the outset, but I did it anyway! And it worked out about how you'd expect – total fail. I would spend an embarrassing amount of time dreading working, then marginally enjoy my patient interactions, followed by even more time to recover. From my easy job! This put my creativity right into the toilet. I was spending so much time dreading or recovering from my "easy job" that I was frittering away the energy meant to pursue my writing dreams. I was so desperate to make money that I kept doing things I hated, making myself sick, and screwing up my desired future in the process.

Yet, it was impossible to see a way out of healthcare for myself that didn't involve a financial meltdown.

When I put my desperation reflex on pause, I was able to appreciate the bigger picture and gain helpful perspective. I had a rainy-day fund in place, so we wouldn't be homeless or starving. At least not in the near future. I would need to make money again at some point, but not immediately. Desperation was landing me in shitty jobs that were killing my creativity. I needed a better plan to get me to my dreams. I needed to go all in on testing out this writing thing and train myself to see the financial outflow as an investment in my future instead of a one way ticket to the poor house. I would be strategic about it and transform my desperation into determination. I had the means and motive to do it, I just needed to close my eyes and jump. In the words of one of my many idols, Sir Richard Branson, "Screw it, let's do it!"

Handle your shit.

Focus

Focus: *the state or quality of having or producing clear visual definition*

"It is very important that we re-learn the art of resting and relaxing. Not only does it prevent the onset of many illnesses that develop through chronic tension and worrying; it allows us to clear our minds, focus, and find creative solutions to problems."

—Thich Nhat Hanh, Vietnamese monk

I think focus can be both helpful and harmful. And focus is absolutely a choice, one we can use to our advantage. I've had to learn to use it in controlled ways—sharpened or softened as the situation dictates. The challenge has been to identify when each is needed and not let one or the other, unchecked, carry me away to unhelpful places. Here's a sample of what this looks like for me:

When I focus too hard on one thing, even if I am sure it is what I really, really want, I may miss out on other opportunities by having tunnel vision.

I can't use my focus to my best advantage when I don't have my priorities figured out. This leads to my attention being hijacked by stuff that doesn't matter that much.

Not focusing strongly enough on my goals prevents me from taking action and making the transition to a different path.

When I focus too much on my negative emotions and what I don't want in life, I don't make any progress. I get stuck.

Sharpen the focus on what could go wrong and I'm less likely to take needed risks to grow.

Softening up the focus on the stuff that freaks me the fuck out helps me to go ahead and do it anyway.

I've discovered that strategically sharpening or softening my focus helps alleviate ALL my varieties of anxiety (and I've got plenty). Here's how this played out in just one (annoyingly persistent) type of anxiety from this journey: financial fears. My nemesis! I was petrified that quitting my perfectly good full-time job was sure to leave me and my family immediately destitute. This was a reflex fear that happened, without my consent, whenever I thought about potentially making very little money for an extended period of time. However, a deep breath and a clear-eyed look at the facts (once I could bring myself to peel my fingers away from covering my eyes) revealed that everything was...well, actually pretty good money-wise. I had no debt, except for a manageable mortgage. Retirement savings and college money for the kids were both in place. And, best of all, I'd saved up a healthy rainy-day fund that would carry me for about a year (if on a budget). All right, life is good!

Not so fast. Anxiety here again. It is incredibly discouraging to watch your emergency fund balance going down, down, down. Savings aren't supposed to go that way! Not in *that* direction! Here is where softening my gaze and not clocking the demise of my dollars with a laser-like focus was helpful. I found that when I quit watching every cent going out so closely, my freakouts (major and minor) occurred less often and were less tenacious.

This careful management of my focus allowed me to function until my brain settled a bit into my new reality. Had I given into my unexamined anxieties about money (and a host of other things!), I would have never moved forward. Often, for me at least, the anticipation and emotions surrounding big changes like this can be paralyzing. Learning to zoom my focus in and out can cause a little vertigo, but, ultimately, it's what allows me to make these big leaps over my own personal hurdles to start living my life in a new way.

Handle your shit.

Resolve

Resolve: *decide firmly on a course of action*

"Resolve and thou art free." —Henry Wadsworth Longfellow

My days in healthcare were clearly numbered. The work that used to feel like a joy, had come to feel like a noose. I had to maintain hope for something better and find a new path. A better path that didn't completely drain my soul.

I wish I could say that once I decided, I mean *really* decided, to get out of healthcare that it was like a light switch turning off one life and turning on another. Yeah, it didn't quite happen that way. I guess it never does. I had no idea where to go. And I had kids in tow! Could I really put myself first and start on a risky road financially while staring down two college tuitions on the very near horizon? Um, yep, guess so. It was just impossible to stay miserable anymore.

The resolve for career change was there, but my future, my new and most excellent career path, was still pretty murky at that time. I had quit full-time healthcare employment which was a big step, but I hadn't completely let go. I was keeping healthcare in my back pocket as my backup, my Plan B, like the ex-boyfriend you keep around for booty calls. I kept the employment search engine Indeed loaded on my phone, *just as a precaution*, I told myself. I scrolled through healthcare jobs for reassurance that I had options whenever I felt uncertain or desperate or convinced this writing thing wasn't going to work out. And by continuing to "just look", healthcare remained there as a possibility and I didn't *really* have to commit to figuring out a whole new direction. I could just flirt with the idea of a new career without having to give up having sex with the ex. It took me a while to see that the inordinate amount of time I was spending on my Plan B was preventing me from going all in on Plan A. Allowing even the possibility of resuming my healthcare career to linger was doing nothing but holding me back (same goes for sex with the ex; more about that in my forthcoming dating and relationships book, so stay tuned. Kidding. Maybe).

I finally realized that the comfort of Plan B was stunting Plan A's growth. I needed to quit thinking small and safe and start thinking big and bold.

One of the scariest things I've ever done was deleting Indeed from my phone. It sounds ridiculous, but it felt huge. Did that mean I never took another healthcare job ever again? No, but it felt like a crucial turning point all the same. To me it signified I was no longer actively looking for, or even willing to entertain the idea of a new career position in healthcare. I might have more plain old jobs in healthcare to stay alive, but never again a career there. I had my eyes where they belonged — on the road ahead instead of behind.

Handle your shit.

Recap

Letting go of my prior identity uncovered a lot of internal and external shit that needed attention if I was ever going to get anywhere. It refused to be ignored. I believe, even though it *is* a touch woo-woo, that the universe does keep sending me the lessons I need to learn until I learn them. In my own time. Like the financial fear stuff (that'll probably be with me forever!). But at least I recognize it and have developed some skills to manage it so that it doesn't completely send me off course anymore. Progress. I have also found that when I start feeling picked on or *victimy*—as in, "Why me?"— it's usually because I am missing something important I need to learn. A cue to pay attention and...

Handle your shit.

Part 3: I Don't Have to Live My Life Like Everyone Else

Walk the Talk

After plenty of soul searching and getting uncomfortably honest with myself, it finally dawned on me in a weird flash of insight (kind of a *duh* moment, really, but stay with me): I don't have to live my life like everyone else! And that means I sure as shit don't have to keep working in healthcare. In fact, I shouldn't. Because if I do, then I learned nothing from those untimely deaths in my family. Or from all those years working with dying people in hospice. Or from how good my divorce turned out. Or from all of the many ways my body is viscerally telling me to leave. Time to walk my talk.

It took some time to get there, but when I finally quit my last full-time healthcare job on October 6th, 2021, to pursue writing mostly full-time it felt momentous. I kept a few small side gigs to keep some dollars rolling in, but this was a critical change in my life. I had taken off the collar, leash, and noose. Cast aside a lifetime of obeying expectations (for the most part). My time was my own. My future was unwritten. It was time to jump in and test the waters!

I don't have to live my life like everyone else.

Acceptance

Acceptance: *the action or process of being received as adequate or suitable, typically to be admitted into a group; the action of consenting to receive or undertake something offered*

"Happiness can exist only in acceptance."

—George Orwell, English author

Acceptance is a tricky thing. We crave it from others and despair when it is withheld. We are taught early on to seek acceptance, to find our comfortable place within society. Probably all of us have had the type of experience of being the last picked when divided up for teams, and it hurts. We care about fitting in and being part of the group. Some of us crave this more than others and none of us *needs* this, but we all care, at least a little bit. It feels good to know where you belong and that you belong somewhere.

Growing up I learned, as most of us do, that it is important to be financially stable, to have a stable job and a stable relationship. Hard to argue with these. However, at heart, I always had a slightly different way of looking at the world, a bit offbeat with a taste for the whimsical and weird. These more unconventional (and authentic) sides of me were humored by my family, but not taken very seriously. What garnered praise was my level head, my good grades, and being so easy to parent. I got the message early on that steady and predictable were the keys to acceptance.

I think it was assumed that I would eventually fall in line and find my place on a traditional career path, and I did. It was easy to get swept up and away by the traditional ideas others encouraged for my life, without ever really asking myself if that was best for me. I wonder what my life would have been like if I had pursued writing and a creative lifestyle from the get-go instead of taking this long detour through stodgy but stable medicine? Or if I had waited longer for the right man? I guess we will never know. However, I do believe that was is meant for you, finds its way to you eventually and this definitely happened for me. But to make way for better things I had to risk my well-established place in my family and society.

What audacity I had to leave a perfectly good marriage (to a doctor!) and a perfectly good career (as a hospice nurse practitioner!). Even though having those things afforded me easy entrance to acceptance, I chafed. Both my marriage and my career were "good" in theory, but neither was deeply fulfilling. I felt a little hollow, even though I fit in.

I figured I was already going off of the rails with my divorce and survived, so why not take another wild-ass risk and quit working full time in healthcare to become a writer? You know...go full-on flaky. And once I did this, I didn't really fit in anywhere predictable anymore.

I kept my career change mostly to myself, and only shared the full story with a trusted few. I didn't have the energy or the desire to manage other people's expectations of me. I didn't even want to risk asking the question *am I accepted for who*

I am now? I didn't want to know and, honestly, I've let go of caring (much) about that outside noise.

But the inside noise was deafening. You'd think, since I was the engineer behind this big ol' life change, that I would have approved of it and accepted it and myself. And there you would be dead wrong. Even when I resisted asking others for their opinions on my actions, harsh thoughts came to me unbidden. I unhelpfully supplied my own judgments that found myself lacking. I'd been well-conditioned to criticize myself for taking risks, being selfish, making moronic financial moves, and leaving a perfectly good career. It got to the point where I didn't even need others to do it for me anymore.

Luckily, a more helpful side of acceptance is growing in me now. The one about recognizing, understanding, and being okay with inevitable change. Accepting the end of my career in healthcare and accepting the end of my marriage both required fighting against that impulse to keep holding on tight, to work it out, to not let all that shared history go to waste. To keep the light of approval from others shining upon me. But I got tired of hanging on to that live, exposed wire of conformity that kept me humming with anxiety. It was only when I finally let go completely and accepted that my marriage and my career were over and accepted myself as I was that things started to get interesting. Even—dare I say it—exciting.

I don't have to live my life like everyone else.

Excitement

Excitement: *a feeling of great enthusiasm and eagerness*

"The biggest lie about getting older is that excitement and growth end with youth."

—Mo The Poet, poet and songwriter

Fear and excitement are two sides of the same coin. One offers a positive and the other a negative spin on change.

I've learned that excitement increases as fear and anxiety are managed and loosen their grip on my dreams. This allows my commitment to my new direction to grow and momentum to build. It's like a rollercoaster (if that's your thing). It's scary when it starts ratcheting upward and you're leaving the safety of the ground, but then as you get closer to the top, it gets more beautiful and thrilling until finally you go over and whoosh down in a fabulous rush.

I remember the first time I was able to allow myself to feel what it might be like to go over the top and no longer work in healthcare. To really let go of my former identity completely—to just let it all fall away, even for just a minute in my mind...and it was fucking magical. I felt a big relief, of course—but something else, something more beautiful than I could ever imagine, was building. The real possibility that I'd never have to go back to working in healthcare again and that I could do something more fulfilling with my life, despite how others might judge me.

There was a moment when I was taking calls on my last day of full-time healthcare work when this thought went through my head: *Is this the last time I'll have to do this—respond to a call and feel like I need to have all the answers? I've spent so much of my professional life building the knowledge and skills to do this work...and I can just let go of all of it? Ahhhh!* It felt surreal. And amazing! Like when I first moved into my own house after my divorce. I'd spent so many years feeling like I was walking on eggshells, never able to let down my guard or totally relax in my own home. But once I finally allowed my marriage to slip away, I was on my way. It was a real turning point when I moved into my cute little yellow house on my own — immediate relief of all the pent up anxiety and frustration I'd been carrying around for YEARS. I didn't fully realize how much continuous stress was inside of me until it was gone. I felt pleasantly heavy in my body—like I was finally grounded instead of floating up in the air, buoyed by constant, jittery anxiety. This was peace at last. I felt like I was where I needed to be, and I started to get excited about what would come next. It felt like a grand adventure was beginning.

Years later the same happened in my work life: as the perpetual anxiety of the job and fear of all the unknowns and what-ifs and what-will-they-thinks associated with my career change washed away, I started to get excited about planning my new direction. *This is really happening! And it's going to be good, so good.*

The more I confront the fear of letting go of things that no longer serve me, including toeing the line of conformity, I've noticed that my fear of change doesn't reach as high or ter- rifying of a peak anymore. Like that rollercoaster hitting the tippy top and then gliding down into joy. There's also less time between those scary peaks as my body gets used to this motion. It's easier to get to the excitement part now that I know what to expect. I'm that girl in the first cart, going over the top, waving my arms up above my head and I don't care how it looks anymore, this is fucking fun!

I don't have to live my life like everyone else.

Guilt

Guilt: *a feeling of having committed some wrong or failed in an obligation*

"Guilt can stop us from taking healthy care of ourselves."

—Melody Beattie, American author

I have hidden much of this fantastic and frightening journey from most of my family, including my teenaged children. I have some guilt about that. I think it's easy to understand why I might have guilt - I mean, you're supposed to share the important stuff in life with those closest to you, right? Let me explain my reasoning.

I have talked about how the family I grew up in does not necessarily welcome coloring outside of the lines when it comes to career. They mean well, but they tend to greet new or "different" plans with lots of probing questions, a little suspicion and a heap of unwelcome advice. I honestly just didn't want to deal with any of that. I did not want to risk having my dream shaped, or possibly even derailed by the expectations of others. They had me somewhat pigeonholed as steady and reliable so I tried to just let them continue to believe that was what I was via the (hopefully) lesser sin of omission.

As for my kids, developmental theory says, and I am para-phrasing here, that teens are all about their friends, fitting in, and figuring out who they are and who they want to be. In short, they are very self-involved at this age, and that is completely normal. You might think that having a mom who is struggling with some of the same identity issues would be relatable, but this is not the case! At least not in in my experience.

Even minimal discussion about me struggling in any way ob-viously upsets them and makes them feel unsafe, unsettled. I find that what my teens need now is to have me there—way, way, way in the background—to support *them* whenever they happen to be ready to talk about their experiences and dif-ficulties. The last thing they want is to hear about mine in any kind of depth. They want me to be stable, solid, safe, predictable; not wrestling with my own demons and upsetting their sense of security. If they were a bit older or even a bit younger, I might have handled this differently, but I choose to keep my experience largely to myself because, developmen-tally, they just aren't equipped to handle it right now. They are way too consumed with figuring out their own shit! Out of respect for their wellbeing, I shield them from my own turmoil, just like I did when I was grieving the loss of my brother and dad. They don't need the full weight of all of this right now.

I guess I could have used kid-related guilt as an excuse to stay stuck in my career (or in my bad marriage), but I didn't. Who knows how long my life is going to be? I don't want to waste any of the precious time I have left. My brother dying at 53 sure as shit brought that one home! So I'm moving forward with my own development while doing the best I can to limit what I share with them kids about this process.

And, in a somewhat ironic twist, I am doing this *for them* even though I am not openly sharing the process as it unfolds *with them.* In many ways they are the inspiration for this life change because I do not want to set an example for them of a person who remains trapped living a life that does not fit. I want to be a better role model than that. Certainly, I answer truthfully whenever they ask directly about any of this stuff, but I find that this rarely happens. They clearly don't want or need to know all the nitty gritty details of my working life struggles and up-and-down efforts to transform myself. They need a mom to blend in with all the other bland, background parents and be there to take care of them now—not the other way around. So while I've kept quiet on the details, I am sure they would have started to notice the growing despair that had become impossible to hide if I had not left my unfulfilling career when I did. Kids don't miss much.

Am I playing this one the right way by keeping many of the people closest to me in the dark? If I were absolutely sure, I'd probably not have these twinges of guilt about it! But, at some point, I had to decide on a course and stick with it, so here we are. I'm hopeful that in the future, we will talk about this time in my life with and what it was like for me. Maybe even when someone is going through something similar and I can be there to encourage them. It won't be a secret forever! I believe now is just not the time. I have other trusted people in my life to support me through this transition, and I am certain my kids and the rest of my family will be proud of me, too—just later. For now, I think this decision is the best path. Fingers crossed.

I don't have to live my life like everyone else.

Validation

Validation: *recognition or affirmation that a person or their feelings or opinions are valid or worthwhile*

"All my big mistakes are when I try to second-guess or please an audience. My work is always stronger when I get very selfish about it."

—David Bowie, English musician

I love this quote—it keeps me honest! Validation is a trap.

Needing the approval of others to feel good about myself or my work is giving too much power away. I know this.

And yet, like most, I crave it at times. Someone, anyone to tell me I'm making good life decisions and that my writing is good, good enough, or at least doesn't totally suck. Someone with a more valuable opinion than my own...oh, wait a minute—that sounds really fucked up! And it is. And I resist the neediness, but it does crop up here and there. Not gonna lie.

Sometimes I read over my words and think, *Damn, that's good!* I *am* the most important critic to please, after all. But I'm also not immune to the need for encouragement or the lure of validation. However, encouragement is not the same as validation, even though the words are sometimes used interchangeably. Validation puts the power in someone else's hands to judge the worthiness of you (or your work). And it's addictive. Often, young kids are taught very early on to seek validation and to never learn to trust their own internal compass. This is tragic. They become little praise junkies, looking for their next fix. Then they grow into adults who are unable to make decisions, make stuff, or make it through life without the reassurance that someone else thinks they're OK.

Encouragement is when someone cheers you on, tells you to keep going without judging. Without making a determination of merit (or lack thereof). We could all use more encouragement in our lives as we grow into more fully self-possessed individuals who know our own minds. I practice this with my kids. When they come seeking validation, I give them a big dose of encouragement instead, and ask them what *they* think about whatever it is they're working on. Helping them internalize this important switch to retaining ultimate creative control over their own lives helps me to do the same myself. Because I *did* grow up as one of those little junkies. Luckily, a great motivator to becoming my better self is knowing that I am a role model for my kids. And they don't miss a trick. Dammit.

So to the book agent who said my book is too short: I think it's perfect, just the way it is.

I don't have to live my life like everyone else.

Freedom

Freedom: *the power or right to act, speak, or think as one wants without hindrance or restraint*

"If you want total security, go to prison. There you're fed, clothed, given medical care and so on. The only thing lacking...is freedom."

—Dwight D. Eisenhower, former United States president

I have never been a great employee, but I am often an excellent worker. What I mean by that is that I get shit done and done well, but I balk at restrictions like timecards, schedules, and micromanagement. I tend to flourish in environments where I have a very long leash. This is probably why I always gravitated toward home-based care. There I could make my own schedule and not be confined by the same four walls all day. I could also avoid small talk—*key* for an introvert like me—and resist getting caught up in petty office politics (which were omnipresent and invariably tiresome). I didn't want to be part of a work family; I just wanted to get the job done as effectively and efficiently as possible so I could get home to my real family. Traffic, mind-numbing and butt-busting windshield time, creepy neighborhoods and occasional sketchy homes to visit were the downsides of the job, but worth it for the relative freedom. And, for many years, this was good enough to keep me going.

But now I crave freedom of the absolute sort. I want control of all my time back. No more punching a timeclock or feeling beholden to an employer. I also don't want to be responsible for others in any kind of direct sense (like being their primary care provider). I want to keep helping people, but not in such an intimate, in-person way. I want distance. I want solitude. I want control of my time. I want to create. On my own schedule.

Sounds like a lot of *want*.

Do I believe I deserve special treatment? Do I think I'm too good for the status quo, the 9-5, the-steady-job-'til-65 plan that most people follow?

No. That's not it.

I have no quarrel with how most folks choose to live their lives. If it works for them, great. I wish them well. I'm not asking for something objectively better, even though there is nothing wrong with wanting that. However, in my case, I just want something *different*. And in that sense, it *will* be better. A better fit. For me.

Giving myself total freedom to be who I really am and not conform to expectations of what it means to be a working adult in America—that is my next real challenge. To leave the familiar shackles for an uncertain future.

I don't have to live my life like everyone else.

Non-Conformity

Non-conformity: *failure or refusal to conform to a prevailing rule or practice*

"Non-conformity is the highest evolutionary attainment of social animals."

—Aldo Leopold, American writer

This is one of my favorite quotes ever! I also love that I discovered it via my page-a-day calendar of quotes when it came up on my birthday last year. How incredibly timely. I've always admired individuals who are boldly unapologetic about being themselves. Many, perhaps unsurprisingly, are rockstars in the true sense of the word: Freddie Mercury, David Bowie, Lady Gaga all come to mind. But there are examples from different walks of life too, like Richard Branson, Roxane Gay, Vivienne Westwood, Anthony Bourdain, heck, even my childhood neighbor Jim Mangio. Jim was a giant and imposing man who dressed everyday in a pair of ragged overalls, gunboat-sized Red Wing boots and was not shy about speaking his mind, often in the most shocking of ways, but always delivered with a devilish grin. He was a real gem, I miss him. What inspires me about all of these people (and there are many others) is how they pushed against the confines of conformity and weren't afraid to live their lives or share their voices in a different, but authentic way. At least that's how it appears.

I have my share of quirks and alternative views of the world, but I've also spent many years being a very successful conformist. And it felt good. Good to be the good girl. Good grades, good college, good career, good husband, good house, good kids. From the outside, I was living the dream. On the inside, I was slowly dying. Being good wasn't good enough. Niggling away at the back of my mind was the sneaking suspicion that this good life that I'd created was not even remotely what I wanted. I desperately tried to ignore it.

I thought I just needed to adjust a few things, move a few levers, spin a couple of dials to make my life work. I moved to a different state, got divorced, tried new jobs, dated, found a fantastic new husband. Most of these were positive improvements in my life. However, the feeling of deep dissatisfaction in my career persisted. As I grew more into myself and tuned into my internal wisdom, it became clear that what I really wanted was a totally different working life.

It took time. I honestly wanted to hide from this realization because it felt too damn hard, but I finally got there. Now I accept that I'm a non-conformist. I desire and thrive within a different kind of lifestyle than the norm. And that's ok. There is nothing wrong with the norm, if that's your thing. It has a lot to recommend it — consistency, stability, social acceptance, a well-defined path to retirement. It's just not for me. I want ultimate authority over how I spend my time. I want to use my creative energy every day, not just nights and weekends after the "real" work is done. I don't want another boss in my life.

There are times when I feel uncomfortable owning this, times when I think to myself, *Who do I think I am quitting a perfectly good career? Why should I get to live my life as I please when everyone else is stuck in the grind? What makes me think I can step out of line, ignore "the rules", and still succeed?* Not at all life or death problems, but painful all the same, and, as such, worthy of attention.

Even in pursuit of a writing career, I'm doing it "all wrong". I'm not taking writing classes, going to workshops, or looking for mentorship. I'm freewheeling this, making up the rules as I go along, writing from my heart, and trying to live up to my own internal ideas and standards about what I think is good stuff to read. It won't be everyone's cup of tea, and that's all right. I'm writing in my voice, in my way, and I'm pleasing myself first.

I have no guarantees of success on this new path—that's certainly true. And there are definitely trade-offs for this much freedom (lack of a steady paycheck to name one). Many people, even ones I love dearly, will likely shake their heads and judge my choices. But none of that's going to hinder me, because I no longer feel the pressure to remain miserable, living someone else's idea of a good life.

I don't have to live my life like everyone else.

Dream

Dream: *a cherished aspiration, ambition, or ideal*

"Dream and give yourself permission to envision a you that you choose to be."

—Joy Page, American actress

I love words. Big words, small words, weird words, odd words, obscure words, 5 dollar words. My kids make fun of me for taking such delight in vocabulary, but I don't care. The shape, sound and meaning of words bring me a lot of joy. I love to express myself through writing, and I always have.

Way back in the third grade, a high point in my life was when I took it upon myself to write a short play about Christopher Columbus, and my peers performed it for the whole class. For fun. Topic choice aside, what kind of crazy kid does that voluntarily? And for fun? And it didn't stop there. Writing papers in high school was the first time I experienced *flow*—being totally consumed and in the moment, in my element. Later, when studying abroad in Belize in the days before mobile phones were omnipresent, I channeled all my cross-cultural travel experience into long-winded, colorful email missives home to my family. They received my words with delight and still talk about them today. Even as a sleep-deprived suburban mom of two tiny kids, I found time to submit a short essay to the local newspaper (remember those?). The editor left a voicemail on my machine (I realize that I am totally dating myself here) saying how it was "journalistically excellent". I played those words over and over again with pride and validation while the spit-up crusted upon my shirt. Writing for fun has been a constant in my life. It also helped sustain me through increasingly dark times in my career and in my marriage. A simple pleasure to distract me from the unpleasantness in other areas of my life.

So why didn't I ever think about pursuing it professionally?

Dreams are all about *what if...* I believe in dreaming big, in aiming high and I am a tireless cheerleader for those around me who are going for it, whatever "it" might be. However, for reasons I'm still exploring, I tend to focus on the negative side of *what if* when it comes to my own dreams. All the stuff that could go wrong, all the holes in the plan, all the perils and pitfalls (whether real or imagined). So when I really let myself dream big for myself, the biggest, baddest career I could think of was to be a writer. But I quickly shut myself down. As I mentioned earlier in this book, writers are rockstars in my world. And, as such, out of reach for mere mortals like me. Excellent, professional writing, the kind you get paid for, must be *hard*. Too hard for me to make a go of it. Right? I mean, I'd at the very least have to go back for more schooling or join some godawful writing workshop in which my peers could gleefully eviscerate my work on a regular basis. *I'm not good enough, it's all out of reach, it's best move on to something else.*

Then there's the happy side of *what ifs*—like the idea that I could leave healthcare and become a successful writer, living my best life. I mean, why *not* me? Those happy sides are definitely there, obviously, but they don't come as naturally to me. Perhaps from an overabundance of practicality and a dearth of self-confidence? I don't know, but, despite this, I kept writing for pleasure even when I didn't dare to dream of any kind of future in it.

As my career became increasingly intolerable, I began writing more. Probably as a means to soothe myself. I started writing about working in hospice and all the crazy, meaningful, and life-affirming stuff that happens there. Then I tried to write about grief and losing my dad and brother, but that wouldn't flow. Still too painful. Maybe in the future it will, but I'm not forcing it. So I started writing reviews of local dive bars, just as a fun joint project with my boyfriend (now husband #2, and the only man for me). The pure joy of this endeavor uncorked my flow and led to writing about cooking, philosophy, life, dating, relationships—a veritable explosion of content. It was like all those years of pent-up frustration, trying to find happiness and fulfillment in a job (and marriage) that didn't fit, were finally released, and it resulted in an enormous tidal wave of creative energy for writing. The flood gates were open!

The more I write, the more I realize that there is no room for compromise or censorship when it comes to dreams. I used to think about how I could modify my dreams to be smaller, to take up less space, to perhaps be more *realistic*. Maybe I could write for medical journals, or patient education materials, or a whole host of other boring-as-shit stuff like that. *Realistic*. What a stupid word. At some point, I just said, *Fuck it. I'm going for this, because what if it works out? I am all in on this dream.* And I am.

I don't have to live my life like everyone else.

Courage

Courage: *strength in the face of pain or grief; the ability to do something that frightens one*

"It takes a lot of courage to release the familiar and seemingly secure, to embrace the new. But there is no real security in what is no longer meaningful."

—Alan Cohen, American author

Damn you, Alan Cohen! Whoever you are. (Apparently, you're an American author, and good for you, but you're pissing me off.)

Kidding. Kind of. I'm sure he's a lovely fellow, but that last bit about having no security in what is no longer meaning-ful—yeah, that hit me where it counts. On closer examination, healthcare is really not the safe, secure haven that I imagined and spent years being afraid to leave. It was a cage. Golden handcuffs I was afraid to take off. Trading my well-being and fulfillment for a paycheck and abuse. Ick. Makes me a bit nauseous even writing those words. It's a difficult thing to acknowledge.

You'd think it would be easy to leave that bullshit behind.

However, I'd be lying if I said that I've totally embraced my new path. I still embarrassingly want to turn around at times, run back and cling to the old, well-worn grooves of working in healthcare rather than even contemplate breaking fresh ground.

This is where courage comes in. It rides shotgun, egging me on to seek out those new opportunities, even though they are scary and risky and unfamiliar. For me at present, fresh ground looks like this: learning to listen to and trust my own intuition. Even when it leads me to places I don't want to go—like quitting a solid job in which I was making the most money of my life. Or risking putting my writing out in public and opening myself up for criticism (and possibly praise?). And, not giving in to desperate impulses to go back, retreat, and resume my solid, joyless career in healthcare. It's also ignoring the cautions of my family and its risk-avoidant culture. Just a lil' sampler of recent instances when I've called upon courage to save me from myself. My weaker self.

What I have learned about courage is that it gets stronger, over time and with practice. Those initial forays into dangerous, unfamiliar territory are fucking hard and scary, though. Sometimes, I rely on memories of past successes to summon courage to my side in the present. Like the time when I confronted an abuser all by myself, all of age 12. My throat felt tight, but my voice was strong when I told him to get out of my room. Or the time when I took a big risk and moved to Belize for three months to work in a charity clinic. What was absolutely overwhelming then, is now a treasured experience. Or when I stood up to that bad boss and quit my job on principle. My hands were shaking, my heart was racing, but my inner philosopher was cheering me on to resist that offense against my internal values. The fact that these scary situations turned into positive ones once I mustered the courage to stand up for myself and take risks helps me feel brave when confronting new tests for myself. I wouldn't say breaking fresh ground is exactly fun—at least not for me—but I do it anyway. Soon, success on my current journey away from my healthcare career and into my writer's life will serve to bring me courage to take on new, future risks. Whatever they may be.

I don't have to live my life like everyone else.

Identity

Identity: *the fact of being who or what a person or thing is*

"Originality consists in trying to be like everybody else—and failing."

—Raymond Radiguet, French novelist and poet

I'm a writer.

Daunting to own that in such a bold, matter-of-fact way. It's much more comfortable remaining in purely aspirational territory. *I wanna be a...*

Action flows most easily from identity, though. Identity also helps with habit formation, a necessity for output as a writer. "I am a writer, therefore I write" helps me overcome inertia in a more helpful way than "If I want to try to be a writer, I should write something". It's a better "why" to get busy on a daily basis. But "writer" wasn't always a part of myself that I recognized.

Historically, my identity in the family and amongst many of my friends was that of the grounded, responsible, wise, sensible one. As the last of six kids, my exhausted parents made no secret of how grateful they were that I was "such an easy child". This kind of identity makes taking any big risks, like getting divorced or quitting a full-time job to pursue a creative career, incredibly unnerving. Unnerving because I'm not sure if those I love will accept this new me. When you are valued for not rocking the boat, it is incredibly scary to make any waves.

I can remember so clearly how my dad, the night before he died in fact, praised me for having created such a good life for myself. I couldn't own it at the time, but I was actually pretty fucking miserable then. When I look back at pictures of myself from that time period, I am struck by how wooden my smile appears, how dead my eyes look. I was lost, but no one, least of all myself, could see it. Then dad died, my world changed and I could no longer brush aside the dysphoria created by my ill-fitting career and marriage. In both cases, I didn't feel like myself anymore. But actually changing my identity to be more authentic to who I was discovering I was underneath everyone else's expectations of me felt like a giant leap. Going from a sane, stable person with a solid job and marriage to one who quits both and welcomes risk in pursuit of a hazy idea of a different, more fulfilling life is a big time shift.

Embracing my new identity meant letting go of the old one. I went through this kind of separation from the old self in my first marriage and find it is just as disorienting in the context of career change. For myself and those around me. Who am I without that husband or that career? Making it even more confusing is the fact that there was a lot to like about that old me. I took some pride in being the respectably married wife of a doctor with two gorgeous kids and a beautiful home in a ritzy suburb of San Francisco. Easy for many to admire. I was also an expert in my chosen field with multiple degrees and lots of professional letters behind my name to prove it. I was someone who put a lot of effort into helping people and was paid very well for it. It felt good to be admired for my career choice. Tell someone, anyone, that you work in hospice and you are pretty much guaranteed some sort of praise. I will miss having such a noble professional identity. Releasing that old identity of "I am a hospice nurse practitioner" means I've had to learn to let go, care a little less, and give a little less of myself to the job, which feels wrong but also necessary.

I'm finding that even when measurable change or progress is made, I don't always appreciate it because I've become so habituated to my old identity. It takes my self-concept a while to catch up to my new reality. This lag can cause discouragement of the "I'll never get anywhere!" variety. I've discovered that writing about myself in the third person when I'm feeling stuck, as if I'm the hero of the story viewed by an outsider, helps me see my progress. "KC bravely left full-time employment to seek a more fulfilling life... There were no guarantees, but she did it anyway..." and so on. These mental gymnastics make my progress easier to see and give me encouragement to keep going. I really am getting somewhere!

Am I comfortable with my new identity as a bold risk taker yet? Hell no! But I'm doing it anyway. As the days go by, I find I sink more deeply into my new persona, and even feel the beginning tinglings of some pure joy. I am learning a lot about myself; the good and the not so great (I can be impulsive, snarky, with more than my share of money hang-ups and a sappy, romantic side when talking about the "universe"), but this clarity allows me to be the most true to myself I have ever been in my life. I'm not sure how this story ends, but I do like who I am becoming, and I am becoming who I like. That is worth the price of admission right there.

I don't have to live my life like everyone else.

Imagination

Imagination: *the ability to produce or simulate novel objects, sensations, and ideas in the mind without any immediate input of the senses*

"The greatest gift that you were ever given was the gift of your imagination."

—Wayne Dyer, American writer

I struggle with imagining myself living my new life. What will that look like? Feel like? How will I get there? Many days it just seems impossible that there will be a time and a world in which I don't work in healthcare. And in which I'm also successful, content, and not destitute and living on the street!

I read a lot of Wayne Dyer when I need a boost. I refer to him as "Uncle Wayne", because he's like the wise uncle in my life that I never had. He encourages those of us pursuing our dreams to practice *feeling* what it will be like to live the life we imagine. This is harder than it sounds!

I can imagine all sorts of desired details about my fantasy future: I'm a successful writer, I get paid a lot of money for my wit and wisdom, I give author readings at Powell's, I enjoy a peaceful, writerly life in my cozy home on my own terms. No time clocks, no commute, no asshole managers. Free to work at 4 a.m. if that's what suits me (and it often does). That is what my dream life *looks* like, but what does it *feel* like? I stretch myself, trying to reach up on my tippy toes for those feelings, but I can't quite grasp them...and then cold, drab reality sets in and I feel discouraged. *I'll never get there.* Soul-level sigh.

Occasionally, I do catch a very brief flash of what I imagine my dream life feels like, and it is overwhelmingly beautiful! Calm and exciting at the same time, filled with ease and confidence and joy. I am warm from the inside out, complete, satisfied. I feel like the best me I've ever been and ever could be in those times.

I'm disappointed that these are currently such fleeting feelings. I want more. I want them to stick around, stay awhile, make themselves at home. How, though? Maybe with practice these feelings will come when I call. Like a loyal dog, brought to heel. Or maybe it's more opportunistic, like making a snowball—when it snows, you get busy right away, gathering up handfuls of flakes, pressing them into a ball that gets bigger and bigger until you have to start rolling it on the ground, where it continues to get bigger and bigger...

I will keep reaching for as many details as I can about how my dream life looks and feels. Gathering up those delicious little bits of joy wherever and whenever I find them until they all finally stick together, forming my new reality—both internally and externally.

I don't have to live my life like everyone else.

Satisfaction

Satisfaction: *the fulfillment of one's wishes, expectations, or needs, or the pleasure derived from this*

"To be able to look back upon one's life in satisfaction, is to live twice." —Khalil Gibran

I spent a long time waiting. Waiting for a safe opportunity to follow my dreams of leaving healthcare for good and doing something creative. Waiting to start enjoying my life instead of slogging away, taking care of everyone else. Waiting for my kids to leave for college. Waiting for my husband to get rich and rescue me from relying on a paycheck anymore. Waiting until retirement. But, most of all, I was waiting for permission that never came. From my ex-husband, my parents, my kids, my friends, society. Basically, from the whole fucking world! I desperately wanted permission from someone—anyone—to stop waiting and to just go for it.

Once I turned 50, I quit waiting. I was tired, burned out on healthcare, and feeling my mortality. Time was slipping away and I found myself on the downward side of life. Is this really how I wanted to go out? On a wave of mediocrity? Dreams untested? Going to a job every day that I'd come to dread? Just plodding ahead toward my golden years?

Nope.

So I gave myself permission to take the time, to go ahead and spend the money I'd saved up for a rainy day. Because it was definitely raining! Pouring, even. And time for me to pursue my own satisfaction. To make my happiness and my dreams my priority. Don't get me wrong: motherhood is my favorite role in life, hands down. I L-O-V-E my kids, and being the best mom I can be is the most important thing I have done (or will do) with my life. I really mean that. And I enjoy all my other roles, too—wife, daughter, sister, friend. I have no plans to abandon these relationships and responsibilities. However, I've held myself in a supporting role long enough, happily and willingly. But now it's my turn to shine.

It's a new concept, but I feel like satisfaction is finally possible for me. *I can have what I want. I can have enough.* No more wanting something other than what I have. No more grudgingly eating almonds when what I really want is Pringles. I can and will have exactly, EXACTLY what I want. What a revolutionary idea! Instead of putting myself off, putting myself last, living for others' dreams and needs and glory, I can have *my own.* I don't have to settle for what is small, sensible, safe, and not too much trouble. I can feel full instead of sadly hollow. I can let go of this core of wanting and actually start *having.*

I don't have to live my life like everyone else.

Recap

The fact that I don't have to live my life like everyone else is my favorite thing I've learned on this journey. Or maybe it's more accurate to say that it's my favorite thing I've *internalized*. By internalized, I mean really accepted something as true, down in my very core, to the point where my thoughts and actions start naturally flowing from it. A big revelation that's come to my attention throughout this experience has been how often my head understands something but my heart lags behind. I have understood, intellectually, that people can be quite successful living all different sorts of lives. I've always appreciated the variety and the endless possibilities. But. *But.* But believing the same is true for me? Much harder to do. Those old, decrepit expectations placed on me as a young person by others (and myself) really have staying power! However, what is different is that now I believe, in my heart and in my head, that this is *also* true for me:

I don't have to live my life like everyone else.

Part 4: Enjoy the Path

Perspective
Matters

Career change has challenged me in multiple ways and on multiple levels, in ways I never expected, but it wasn't all a drag. Once I started writing and taking better care of myself, my wounds began to heal, and slowly, *slowly*, I began enjoying my life again.

And then my personal and professional lives diverged in the most unexpected of ways. While I might have been struggling mightily to figure out my shit with work, my dormant love life began to flourish. The divorce that had rocked my world and made me feel like a loser also made me wiser. Things I learned from my failed marriage made me better prepared to find true love later. Anyway, it didn't happen all at once, and there is a whole story there about what needed to happen for me to be in a place where finding love was possible. I plan to write about that life changing adventure in my next book, tentatively titled *Desperately Dating*. But, long story short: I totally won the love lottery. Three years after my divorce, I joyously remarried. Was a relationship necessary to enjoy my life? Of course not. In fact, just before I met my now-husband, I had resigned myself to a life without a great love story. I was honestly at peace with that because I knew I could be content and live a full and happy life without that experience. Was a partner necessary for my continued personal growth? No again, and certainly not! I would have gotten there (here) eventually, but, in my case, it absolutely sped things along. Having a caring, supportive partner does wonders for personal growth. And eases the pain of falling out of love with a career. I highly recommend it.

But getting my love life right was a process, and it required initial heartache and effort to process ugly feelings before paying off. Turns out, career change does, too. The pursuit of growth is often difficult and messy, but also beautiful. If you look at it in the right ways.

Enjoy the path.

Risk

Risk: *to expose to hazard or danger; possibility of loss or injury*

"Be willing to be uncomfortable. Be comfortable being un-comfortable. It may get tough, but it's a small price to pay for living a dream."

—Peter McWilliams, American author

When I first started flirting with the idea of leaving healthcare and really making a go of being a writer (like for reals), I had to overcome some serious risk aversion. All my life I've internalized the values of safety and security and stability. For as long as I can remember, the writer dream was relegated to the category in my brain of "just a dream; safer to remain as untested potential than to try and risk failing". I had little desire to risk proving, to myself and to others, that I don't have it. That I'm devoid of worthwhile talent. Ugly, but true feelings.

The flipside of course, involves even more risk: if I don't go for it, I might be missing something amazing. Missing the joy of living fully as myself, doing what I love everyday instead of what merely sustains me. And possibly...rocking it?

Neither risk was particularly palatable.

Looking back to the point in time when I finally made the agonizing decision to let go of trying to save my dying marriage brought me some comfort. I was afraid of the risk then, too, of making a change to benefit myself and myself alone. One that would certainly be hard for others to accept (kids, family, friends). However, it became intolerable for me to continue being so lonely and unhappy in my marriage. I was scared leaving, but it had gotten to the point where I had no other option than to chuck it all and risk a new path. I am *so* glad I did! The amazing, beyond-belief outcome of that earlier experience of successfully confronting risk brought me courage when I stood on a career cliff that felt just as scary.

But I did it. I left full-time employment in October 2021 to give the writing thing a real shot. It took a little while to get the wheels in motion, but soon I hit my groove and was churning out content like nobody's business.

As I built up confidence, I slowly let every one of my side hustles in healthcare fall away. And there I stood, 6 months later in the spring of 2022, completely separated from my old career. Almost without noticing it, I had quietly evolved away from my deep, deep risk aversion by consistently taking small steps toward the new. I was patting myself on the back for this and for realizing that the anticipation of making a big career change—much like when I was contemplating divorce—was WAY worse than actually doing it. So I was chugging along on this new path, feeling pretty pleased with myself, all of my focus on writing and starting to get excited about possibilities. I was loving living my life as a writer, but then...

As you might have guessed, healthcare started trying to reel me back in.

Just as I was getting comfortable in my life without healthcare: not one, not two, but *three* different employers came calling within *one week*. I was being tempted left and right with job offers that had flexible scheduling, offered lots of money, perks and appeared to require relatively minimal effort. Some of these jobs even seemed "perfect", thereby feeding the deep seed of doubt within me that *knew* I'd have to go back to my healthcare career someday anyway.

Just like in many break-up stories, my divorce was called off once, and I don't regret that. We tried to work out our shit, but, ultimately, we weren't successful. There is no shame in that. There was a lot riding on our marriage, and two very special little kids to consider. We had to be *sure* sure that divorce was the right answer for us. Same with my career. Was I really ready to let go?

I entertained the idea of giving my healthcare career one more shot, turned it over in my mind, imagined the feeling of relief I'd have being safely employed again and making some real money. I gave myself reasons, really good reasons, to take one of those jobs:

—won't hurt to make some money...

—these job opportunities are coming for a reason, and you'd be a fool to pass them up...

—working a little now could will keep your hand in the game for when you fail at this writing thing later...

And on and on and on. If I sound conflicted about all of this, that's because I was. And unwittingly trying all sorts of ways to justify putting the collar and leash back on and staying *safe*. In reality, trying very hard to sabotage myself. I must *really* need to learn this lesson about overcoming risk aversion, because it keeps popping up in my life with such stubborn regularity!

In the end, I had a little fun with it all and took the opportunity to beef up other aspects of my risk tolerance muscle. Being socialized as a woman of my generation, salary negotiations have always been uncomfortable. It is hard to ask for what I am worth—and that's embarrassing to admit, but true. I'm not a total shrinking violet on this front however, but I did feel like I pulled some punches over the years in certain situations to maintain my status as a "good girl". Puke.

And the healthcare system, which employs mostly women, capitalizes on this learned weakness in many of us who were taught not to be greedy or bold or difficult. It encourages us to be martyrs to the cause while they pay us less and work us more, which is utter bullshit. OK, I digress, but here's the thing: in this case, I wasn't desperate. I had figured out how *not* to have a job for a while. These employers came looking for *me* and I gave zero fucks. I had nothing to lose, and so I negotiated like I'd always dreamed of doing. I was calm and matter of fact while I owned my expertise and firmly asked for big money. Huge money! Money to match my value, dammit. I made demands, I said no to shit I didn't want to do anymore, and asked for every other benefit I could think of, just to see what would happen. It felt good to be so relaxed about the process, so in control. My terms or no deal.

As I saw it, if they were willing to give me everything I asked for, then maybe I should take a real look at the opportunities on offer. I'm a dreamer, but I'm practical, too. I decided to play it out and see if any of the positions suited me well, on my terms —which meant not a career or full-time position, no supervisory responsibilities and definitely no set schedule. I had new standards!

There was no pressure to take a healthcare job at that point, but I was warming to the idea that I just might benefit from a final gig, a swan song of sorts.

Enjoy the path.

Integrity

Integrity: *the state of being whole and undivided; the quality of being honest and having strong moral principles.*

"To give real service, you must add something which cannot be bought or measured with money, and that is sincerity and integrity."

—Douglas Adams, English author

Providing healthcare to humans has been an honor. I still believe in hospice and its mission. Dying people deserve respect, expert care, and support. Even if I, personally, have come to feel disenchanted with this work, it is still good work. I just don't want to be the one to do it anymore.

There have been times when I was ready to quit healthcare out of anger or frustration. Other times from paralyzing ennui or deep, deep depression and fatigue. I've felt burned out, burning to leave, and, sometimes, just burned. Ultimately, when I finally made my final big break from full-time employment, I just sort of slunk away under a dark cloud of disillusionment.

I thought that was that—end of story, bye-bye healthcare career. However, I didn't feel great about my exit. It felt anti-climactic, angry, unsettled, and just a little bit sordid. It didn't sit well.

But I was on to better things.

However, healthcare wouldn't let go.

And that's when I realized that it was important to me to have a clean break. I wanted to leave on good terms, the right way, with my integrity intact.

My deep-seated risk aversion ironically provided me the means I needed. Even though I'd "left" healthcare as a career for good, I still worried about money all the time—especially when I wasn't making any. When recruiters came a-callin', I felt compelled to at least have a listen to what they were offering. Kind of weak in one sense (not very courageous or committed to my resolution to leave, was I?), but this foible of mine ended up bringing me the perfect opportunity to leave on a high note.

I was courted to provide staff education for a hospice on a part-time, contract basis and I jumped at it. Here was a chance to pass on some of the knowledge and wisdom I'd gained over my career and help prepare the next generation of hospice staff to carry on the work. And I would have no direct clinical responsibilities myself. Sigh of relief. This finally felt *right*. Here was a way forward without being completely sucked back in to my dead career. A way in which I could leave a little less abruptly, on a positive note, providing a final act of service and with my head held high. Helping the next generation carry the torch forward while I slip away into a different life.

Enjoy the path.

Ease

Ease: *to make (something unpleasant, painful, or intense) less serious or severe*

"Being at ease with himself put him at ease with the world."

—John Steinbeck, American author

Ease is my overarching goal in life. And I'm not looking for or expecting an "easy" life, because I believe effort is required for good things and progress. I mean "ease" more in the sense of having a calm, peaceful relationship with the important people in my life, with my work, and with myself. I think this concept is so vital to my own personal definition of success, because I have experienced exactly the opposite: a global lack of ease. My marriage sucked, my job sucked, and I didn't like who I'd become.

In October 2021 I was navigating away from my healthcare career without the benefit of a full time job or a clear view of a new destination. I felt the *opposite* of ease. I was really uncomfortable being basically unemployed and living off of my savings. I felt I needed some success to validate the decision to leave full-time employment, like *right the fuck now.* So I constructed a strict, daily writing schedule, even set alarms to keep myself honest, and basically tried to force myself into a brand-new box. Awake at 4:44 a.m. (I like the number 4), yoga and meditation with a cup of tea, and then writing from 6-8, breakfast with the kids between 8-830, at the gym by 9, home writing again by 11, and so on. I hated it! My desperation and rigidity, unsurprisingly, did not lead to great creative output! Just the opposite, in fact.

Even though I was no longer overburdened with work stress and busyness, I was making myself miserable! I'd gotten it into my head that work *must* be hard and unpleasant, so was unconsciously re-creating those kinds of conditions. I was trying to go from my old, deeply ingrained reality straight into my new one, with no allowance for a transitional phase. No rest, no recovery, no reflection. Yeah, that was a dumb idea.

So I chucked it all and experimented with the other extreme: no plan, no schedule, no alarms, no *shoulds*. I set a bottom-line savings number I was willing and semi-comfortable with spending down to, and encouraged myself (with mixed results) to put making money out of my mind for the following six months. I gave up any daily expectations for myself. If I felt like writing when I woke up, I wrote, and if I didn't, I tried not to stress about it. I just did what I wanted to do every day and tried to enjoy my time. For the most part, I succeeded.

After about two months of this no-routine routine reset, I found that I had a lot to say. Words and ideas started pouring out of me. I'd wake up with ideas ready to go and my book, *this* book, started writing itself a couple of hours per day, every morning. I was back in the flow again. Content was everywhere, coming out of my pores. I guess I just needed a rest to recover and heal from leaving healthcare, but I was finally rocking this writing thing. At the same time, I was enjoying my home life and feeling more fulfilled as a human than I ever had. The initial panic about lack of income and direction subsided, and I started to feel relaxed, calm, and peaceful with this decision.

What I took away from this experience was that what I needed to successfully leave both my first marriage and my first career was distance, time, rest, and the experience of the ease I'd been missing in both. In these situations, I learned that the paralyzing fear of the unknown—of leaving safety, familiarity, and rigidity behind—eventually lets up and the sun shines again. Ease is possible and new possibilities emerge as a result.

I'd found my groove. Or so I thought.

And then March 2022 arrived. I was depressed the whole month. I wrote (with great effort) a total of maybe three chapters of my book (and my chapters are really short) and a couple of travel articles. Not much, not even a fun dive bar article, and those usually perk me up. I felt listless, unmotivated, fatigued with low-level anxiety about my general lack of engagement with life. The *opposite* of ease. Again. WTF? How and why had my love train derailed all of a sudden?

By the end of that shitty month of power journaling, tons of TV, and angst, I was starting to shape an answer.

What I've come to understand is that ease is meant to be progressive. The first taste of ease after a long absence (whether in a marriage or a career) is intoxicating. *I can finally rest! Life doesn't need to be such a struggle all of the time! I am so grateful! I've made it!* Cortisol levels drop, peace levels rise, and that omnipresent anxiety finally takes a hike. Eventually, though, the experience of this initial ease runs its course and you're left with a future ahead that you have to figure out. The key is this, though: definitely enjoy that novelty of newfound ease and allow it to start to heal you. However, don't expect it to sustain you for the rest of the journey. It is not built to last. You must use it as a foundation to build the new life that you *really* want.

Being job-free after leaving a career that had run its course was such a relief! Just like when I left my first marriage and moved into that cute little house, alone. I hadn't realized how much constant anxiety I was carrying until I finally set it down and found peace again. But that relief, unsurprisingly, didn't last—in either situation. It wasn't meant to. It was a recovery way station, but since I didn't really want to remain single or job-free forever, I had to get moving again. Regarding the job situation, March shook me awake and told me it's time to get on with it. *Find your future.*

And that has been the hard part. Without external forces to guide me, to tell me where to go, what to do when and for how long — time just stretches out ahead in a disconcerting, shapeless, infinite line. It's all up to me. It is entirely my responsibility to figure out how to give my own life meaning and shape without relying on others or a predetermined path to tell me what to do. Oh sure, there are the daily necessities, but after the food has been cooked and consumed, dishes washed, laundry folded, and dog walked, what comes next? I can only read so many books that have been lingering on my shelf or watch so many episodes of those period dramas I love before I start missing some structure to my days and accomplishments to earn my rest at night. I don't like (and have never liked) being told what to do, but can I figure out how to tell myself what to do to reach my writerly goals without inciting internal rebellion? Can I truly find sustainable ease in my work life, and by my own design?

I think, ideally, that initial ease becomes the firm footing from which to hope and strive for something better. I want to put that ease to work for myself and yoke it with achievement, with progress. Ease is the absence of conflict, but that's not the full meaning or capacity of the word. There is another, more elevated stage of ease that lives in the flow: that feeling when you are doing your thing (whatever it is), it's going great, everything is clicking, progress is being made, and you feel peaceful and fulfilled. *That's* what I want for my future. Absence of conflict is not enough. I want to push through that to the other side of ease—ease 2.0—where things get really great. I'm not there yet, and that's all right, because I've come to understand the value of appreciating where I am. I've made the important first step of leaving healthcare as a career, and that is progress and brings a certain peace all on its own. I am moving in the right direction, and I feel better because of it. However, I also know that I would be foolish to stop here, even though it is pleasant, because *great* may be just a little bit further up ahead.

Enjoy the path.

Impatience

Impatience: *eager restlessness*

"Youthful impatience obscures the endless potential for joy that's standing right in front of you."

—Greg Gutfield, American TV host

It was a process, often painful, but now I know what I want for my new career path. So why can't I just get there already? I am incredibly impatient at this point.

I want to be published so badly that I can taste it. This has been a fucking marathon and I can see the finish line.

I know I have a tendency to start rushing when I begin to tire of a project, usually when I'm close to completion. I just want it to be DONE. This project—this book—is no different.

But I don't want to blow it here at the end.

So many months of writing, so many words (even if one book agent out there thinks there are too few), pouring so much of my soul out here onto these pages. Learning painful truths about myself and lessons required to grow. So much emotion, deep stuff welling up and out, internally processed and printed here for all to see. To judge. But, hopefully, to benefit from wisdom gained and shared.

I can't fuck it up now.

Counterintuitively, at least to me, I've learned to stop writing when I feel impatient and tempted to rush. I force myself to take a break from it. I do something else, stuff I enjoy: watch bad TV, plant stuff, cook up a storm, or think about new book ideas. Have cocktails with my husband on the patio and listen to Frank Sinatra. Go out to lunch with my mom. Walk my dog. Let my son practice driving me around and listen to him talk about his love for cars. Play with my daughter's hair while she's flopped in my lap and savor this time because she's leaving for college in two short months.

I don't want to wish my present away by being so focused and driven to reach my future. There is joy and richness right here, right now. The future will surely arrive in its own time, but *the path* is where it's at. My new career is not like my old one, no longer do I rush through the days so that I can get back to living my *real* life, the one that matters. I am a writer now, and my lifestyle accommodates my life and the people in it. I can take my time and enjoy it.

Enjoy the path.

Funk

Funk: *a state of depression*

"Creativity is an act of magic rising up from your subconscious. It feels wonderful every time it happens, and I've learned to live with the anxiety of it not happening over long periods of time."

—Bruce Springsteen, American musician

An emotional funk (not to be confused with the most excellent musical genre) isn't a deep, deep depression. It's more like depression light, or a depression snack. A brief, bitter taste of when things all of a sudden go from bright technicolor to shades of grey. When these most unwelcome funky feelings appear, my creative light flickers and I worry when it dims that maybe it has left me forever. *That's it. It was a good run, but it's over and you've had all of the good writing you will ever get.* This may sound melodramatic, but believe me, it is oh-so-real in my heart.

Even though I know in my head that I probably just need to ride it out with some extra rest for a few days, the world looks fucking bleak in these times. In fact, I'm trying to write this right now while in a funk, and it sucks. Nothing is flowing, my words seem artless and clunky, everything is effortful and unsatisfying. *Ugh. I'm terrible at this.*

Sometimes, I imagine my funks as storms blowing through—like an unexpected rainy day smack-dab in the middle of summer (I live in Washington state, mind you, the rain capital of the world so that shit happens). When I think of it in these terms, it helps me settle in and enjoy the grey instead of lamenting it, worrying it, dreading it. Stay cozy, be kind to yourself. It'll pass.

Enjoy the path.

Peace

Peace: *freedom from disturbance; tranquility*

"Nobody can bring you peace but yourself."

—Ralph Waldo Emerson, American philosopher

My peace has been tested in surprising ways during this migration away from my former life. The absence of conflict has, surprisingly, taken some getting used to. Daily friction from my ill-fitting career and all that it brought to my daily existence is now absent and I have the freedom I always sought. So why does it feel so uncomfortable and like I'm waiting for the other shoe to drop? Maybe I don't know how to live in peace?

My peace was constantly tested in my life as a nurse practitioner: traffic, bad bosses, evil insurance companies, adorable but clueless patients, constantly juggling mom life and work life while walking a tightrope over a yawning canyon of despair threatening to swallow me whole on a daily basis. Now, *that* was living! Drama, tension, good fights and bad fights, but never a dull moment. And now I don't have those things to fight against anymore and I feel...well, a bit lost. There's no longer anything external to blame for my unhappiness. So where do I go from here?

Now, the biggest threat to my peace is when the logjam of ideas refuses to pass and I wonder if my creativity will ever start flowing again (it always does, eventually). I guess worry is a dependable disturber of my peace. Good ol' worry will never forsake me and his job is never done. I can still worry about making money, the environment, animal cruelty, world peace, and what my neighbor thinks about my lackadaisical approach to the weeds overtaking her view of my side yard (sorry, Danielle). Worry allows me to avoid figuring out how to live with peace. Peace is unfamiliar and maybe a tad...boring?

Boring, perhaps, but undeniably good for my health. My blood pressure is fantastic, my stress hormone levels are way down, my time spent on exercise is up, and I'm sleeping the best I have in years, maybe decades. I have more interest in sex again (my husband likes this one). I make my kids breakfast to order every morning and fun snacks to greet them with after school (they like this one). I read for pleasure again, not just for work. My dog is thrilled to have me home all the time to serve as his support animal. I say yes a lot more to the important people and activities in my life, because I'm no longer too busy, too tired, or too stressed out to find time for them. Peace definitely has its pluses! And these are what motivate me to figure it out—figure out how to live with peace now that it is here. Ahhh, there's my old familiar friend friction showing up again—so glad to have you back.

Enjoy the path.

Dread

Dread: *to feel extreme reluctance to meet or face*

"When fear makes your choices for you, no security measures on earth will keep the things you dread from finding you. But if you can avoid avoidance—if you can choose to embrace experiences out of passion, enthusiasm, and a readiness to feel whatever arises—then nothing, nothing in all this dangerous world, can keep you from being safe."

—Martha Beck, American author

Fuck you, dread. Get outta my head.

I'm nearing the end of writing my book and here comes dread—*again*. Despite my best efforts to lean into this time away from full-time work and enjoy my freedom living my dream life—as a writer—the dread of going back to work as a healthcare provider won't seem to budge. I am dreading putting this book out into the world and having it fail to find an audience. Not because I want to be famous or rich or validated by others' approval (although I'd accept these, if I must!). But because failure to sell this book will mean I may have to go back to where I don't want to go, to a life I no longer want to live. I so want this book to succeed as a harbinger for a new career as a writer for me. I want a new identity from it. I want to be a published author.

I know there is nothing wrong with wanting these things. My fear is I might allow desperation to creep in, take over and ruin my shot at reaching my dream life. It's okay to *want* it, but once you start feeling like you *need* it, then you're fucked. Bad decisions made out of desperation follow and then the whole train derails. I'm careful to keep myself on track as best I can by holding these things lightly.

And yet, failure seems certain. Just a matter of time until my happy, maybe even happiest, time is up. Dumb dread.

Dread is about the future. About what may or may not come to pass. It gets in the way of living in the present. Seems obvious to just give it the boot and enjoy the now, but I find that easier said than done. My dread is sticky. Like gum on my shoe that refuses to lose its irritating gumminess that I feel with every step. Will I ever feel like I am "safely" away from my old life in healthcare? Or will it always be lurking there in the shadows, waiting to snatch me back? What's it gonna take? Time? Success? Money? What is the antidote to dread? I wish I knew.

I hope I get to know. I want to.

Enjoy the path.

Gratitude

Gratitude: *the quality of being thankful; readiness to show appreciation for and to return kindness*

"If you see no reason to give thanks, the fault lies in yourself."

—Tecumseh, Shawnee chief and warrior

Everybody talks about the importance of gratitude. *Yawn.*

It's an overplayed song, but that doesn't make it any less true. I'm gonna include it, but I'll try to skip the trite stuff.

I am grateful every day and for every thing—no exceptions. OK, maybe momentarily trite, but bear with me.

I appreciate how much I have going for me, and I also appreciate everything that has gone against me. Both, together, make up the richness of my life.

I've had a lot of advantages in life. I was raised in a stable home, I've always enjoyed good health and I got an excellent education. I'm white and reasonably attractive and I've seen some of the world. I am deeply grateful for all of these things and that have certainly made my life easier.

That being said, I wouldn't be where I am now, undertaking a huge life change, if I hadn't gone through my share of shit. Losing my dad and brother in 2013 definitely tops the shit list, followed closely by my painful divorce two years later. Those shitty things rocked and rattled my world, but also spurred me on, shook me out of my complacency, and propelled me toward a more fulfilling life. For that I am eternally grateful. Even if, at the time, those events seemed cruel and unfair.

A lot of personal growth has occurred on this journey away from my old career. Old and deep hurts have been dredged up, recognized, acknowledged, and healed. Not exactly fun, but I am grateful for the growth and the opportunity to know myself more deeply and to become the *me-est* me I can be.

I am grateful to those who accept and encourage me on this journey. And to those that don't. Both strengthen my resolve and (re)direct me toward what really matters in any, but especially creative, endeavors: my own approval.

But gratitude has a dark side, too. It can be used as a weapon or tool of control when wielded by others (or oneself) to shame. *What do you have to complain about? Be happy with what you've got.* I have experienced this, and it is confusing and painful to feel wrong for wanting something different. Not necessarily *more*—just different. It is not up to others to determine what is acceptable for me and what makes me happy. They aren't living my life. Shaming myself or allowing others to talk me into accepting and being grateful for things that leave me feeling mediocre is tragic. I will do my best to resist.

I'm grateful for the opportunity I'm giving myself to correct my course, get it right, and pursue the life of my dreams. Every minute of the journey has been valuable.

Enjoy the path.

Overwhelmed

Overwhelmed: *buried or drowning beneath a huge mass; completely defeated*

"Sound character provides the power with which a person may ride the emergencies of life instead of being overwhelmed by them. Failure is...the highway to success."

—Og Mandino, American author

The idea of writing a book—a whole book!—was and is completely overwhelming. Undertaking a project of this magnitude while willfully underemployed, raising two teenagers, and helping out my mom who has a debilitating chronic illness is a lot. I also happen to be going through menopause (I'm always hot, I can't sleep, and my mood swings are epic. Get out of the way). During a global pandemic. With college expenses looming on the horizon in the midst of a stock market crash. Not to mention all of the other business-of-living stuff that I gotta do on a regular basis to keep this ship afloat (cooking, cleaning, yard work, managing finances, paying bills, and on and on). Fun times!

No wonder I feel completely overwhelmed by life on occasion.

But still I question why I am so tired when I "shouldn't" be, since I'm not even working full-time. But you know what? This shit is exhausting. There's always something I "should", or at least, could, be doing.

And then I also wonder why the creativity isn't there sometimes when I sit down to write. Well, duh. Life demands a lot!

I'm actually surprised that I've managed to finish this book. A lifelong dream. Yeah, how the fuck did I even do that?

I broke it down into small, doable parts is how. I kept a soft focus so that my anxiety about what I was doing wouldn't run away with me. I didn't think about writing a whole book or for an audience; I just wrote short, freewheelin' vignettes to express myself and my experience in an honest, authentic way. I tried to lean into the excitement instead of giving into my fear of failure. And of success. Sometimes I'd make myself show up and at least do a little—and sometimes it turned into a lot. Sometimes not. I believed that it was possible and important to respect my desire to take care of everyone and everything in my life, but to not use that as an excuse to avoid pursuing my own dreams. At the same time. I tried not to freak out. Too much. Or for too long. And I tried to be kind to myself. Even when I was tired, pathetic, sad, and overwhelmed. Or when my writing was less than perfect. Sometimes good enough is good enough. At least I was headed in the right direction and *that* felt great.

Enjoy the path.

Self-Compassion

Self-compassion: *acting the same way towards yourself when you are having a difficult time, fail, or notice something you don't like about yourself as you would toward others you care about*

"Self-compassion is a more effective motivator than self-criticism because its driving force is love, not fear."

—Kristin Neff, associate professor of psychology at the University of Texas

I did not grow up with self-compassion as a family value. I had to learn it later. Almost out of desperation to save myself, my sanity. My family of origin taught me all about stoicism. *Feeling bad for some reason? Don't dwell on it—force yourself to get over it. Think of something else (and it will go away).* Taking time to process or understand emotions wasn't even a thing. *Just kick yourself in the ass and move on.* And then there was the self-flagellation part. I remember so many times watching my dad absolutely brutalize himself, out loud, in the most innocuous of circumstances. Like calling himself a horrible loser (using much more colorful language than that) over something pretty benign, like missing a putt on the golf course. This was confusing to me because he was incredibly kind and encouraging to us kids, but unbelievably harsh on himself. I guess the message I internalized was I had to be a strict, unloving disciplinarian to myself at all times.

I wish this were not true.

I wish I'd learned to comfort myself effectively earlier in my life. I went through a lot of unnecessary heartache because of it. I have had a range of difficult challenges (like all people do). Mine include childhood sexual abuse, depression, friend betrayal, an ill-fated marriage, deaths, divorce, and the end of an unfulfilling career path. I survived these, but at what cost? I learned to ignore my feelings and numb the more stubborn ones that wouldn't be forced away. Rather than solace, I offered myself heaps of criticism. This was not sustainable. But it was all I knew. I was always able to handle the basics of daily living, and I looked strong and capable on the surface, but my poor coping crutches were rubbing my skin raw underneath. There had to be a better way.

My divorce was a turning point. I spent much time examining what had gone wrong in our marriage—what was my part, what was his part, where did I need to grow and what did I need to learn to be successful in future relationships? I read a lot of books. I did a lot of thinking. I took a deep dive below the surface of all of my numbed-out feelings and memories. There was a lot of shit down there that was affecting my mental health. It needed to be brought to the surface for processing and healing. I knew no one would or could do that for me, except for me.

I read something somewhere that talks about how your heart heals only when you give it the time, space, and love to do so. I started practicing this. Instead of immediately turning away or reaching for ways to distract myself or deaden my difficult feelings and memories, I sought them out, welcomed them in, gave them silly names, made friends with them, heard their tales of woe. I guess I learned to nurture myself.

Self-compassion tells us it's okay to take at least as good of care of ourselves as we do everyone else. This concept has helped me let go of a lot of unhelpful programming. I accept now that it's normal to feel bad when bad stuff happens. I also know that I need to process that shit or it will fester under the skin and come out in unexpected, damaging ways. If I don't make my own well-being a priority, who will? My spouse? Kids? Friends? Employer? My mom?

Nope. This one is all on me. This means, when I am feeling scared or tired, I am kind and reassuring to myself that it is ok to have unpleasant feelings. Or to have a rest and not be busy all of the time.

I think some people, even some from my history, may see this as a bunch of self-indulgent crap. So be it. I enjoy feeling whole, in touch with myself in a way I never was before. I no longer feel afraid of my feelings with the urge to immediately suppress them. We can peacefully coexist. I can listen and respond and be nice to myself just as I do for those I love. I am worthy of kindness and care.

Enjoy the path.

Contentment

Contentment: *a state of happiness and satisfaction*

"Health is the greatest gift, contentment the greatest wealth,
faithfulness the best relationship."

—Buddha

I am content. I believe I am content now because I have uncovered and learned how to live in harmony with my deepest held,
core beliefs. Even when going through something as scary,
disorienting, and demanding as a career change, I now realize
how much I rely on these values and convictions:

Life is too short to be miserable.

Handle your shit.

Enjoy the path.

I don't have to live my life like everyone else.

I know how to act, how to react, how to understand whatever is going on in my life through the lens of these beliefs. In my experience, when I attend to these values and let them guide my decision making, I am golden. It's when I allow other voices to distract me from my own path to contentment that shit goes awry.

Curating is key for keeping myself on track. Cutting out those duties, people, jobs, and voices in my head that conflict with my values and prevent me from reaching contentment. Sometimes it's easy and satisfying, like when I quit that job, the one where the boss didn't stick up for me when I was being publicly bullied by a male superior. Yeah, fuck that. Life is too short to be miserable. And that paralysis that kept me working in healthcare jobs long past my expiration date? That paralysis provoked me to figure out how to handle my shit and learn how to quit wasting my precious time on fear.

Other times, though, it's much less straightforward. At one point, I thought that starting my own healthcare consulting and advocacy business would honor my tenet to enjoy my path. If I could just work for myself and didn't have to be a clinician or deal with insurance companies anymore, maybe I could stay in healthcare and be content. That was a big fucking fiasco! I was totally fooling myself and trying to get out of having to do the harder thing (leaving my established career) with a safer pivot. But it was a dead-end path I needed to walk before circling back to insistent reality: I wanted out of healthcare *completely*. Because life is too fucking short to be miserable and I was FAR from enjoying my path.

I was forced to confront myself about how long I'd been stifling my own voice. I overstayed in my healthcare career (and in my marriage) because I was willing to make others' opinions more valuable than my own. I accepted being unhappy and unfulfilled because I was a coward. I was afraid of the fallout and of how my decision to do what it would take to make myself happy and content might be judged harshly by others. I was afraid to potentially be seen as selfish, irresponsible, and flaky. So I stayed. And suffered. But not anymore. Now it is clear that what appears to be the easier thing (staying) is actually the harder thing, because it fucks with every single one of my core beliefs. And who cares what anyone else thinks? I don't have to live the same life as everyone else. Contentment entered the picture when I committed to learning, believing, and living the four truths at the top of this chapter—*my* truths.

Enjoy the path

Epiphany

Epiphany: *a moment of sudden revelation or insight*

"When you come to the realization that the only person who you need to make happy is yourself, your entire life will change and it will become what you always wanted it to be."

—ACM the poet, South African artist

One day, it dawned on me. It was a fucking epiphany.

I *am* living the life I wanted. Right here, right now. This is it—I am *doing* it! This is how it feels to live the life I want. Of course, there's a shitty little voice in my head that sometimes likes to point out that I have yet to make a dollar from my writing and that is true, but...

But.

In this moment, I have everything I need and want.

I am living a writer life. I am producing content that pleases me and meets my own internal standards. I write about what interests me. I no longer work full-time as a healthcare provider. My time is unscheduled. I work when and where I want for as long as I want. I can (and do) go for walks or do whatever else I want in the middle of the day; nobody is monitoring my use of my own time anymore. I am comfortable financially (for now). I have brain space and heart space for the things that matter to me. I am present as a parent, a sister, a daughter and as a spouse. I am content. I am free. I am really enjoying my life. I'm going to celebrate this and gently guide myself to focus on this moment instead of dreading the end of it. To enjoy it. To get used to how this feels, because it is my present and my future.

Enjoy the path.

Recap

Enjoying the path definitely falls under the heading of "easier said than done". But just because something is hard, doesn't mean it isn't worth doing. Just because I'm in the midst of a life change doesn't mean I can't or won't enjoy the process. I don't believe that there's wisdom in putting off joy, peace, contentment, or allowing myself to be consumed by fear, anxiety, or shame. I've learned to name my emotions instead of numbing them. No matter how noble or grand the distant goal is, my life is what I do every day and how I do it. I've come to understand that it is prudent to enjoy it as much as possible along the way.

Enjoy the path.

What Does It All Mean?

Healthcare is good work; it's just no longer the work for me. Falling out of love with my career was a process just like falling out of love with my first husband: It didn't happen all at once, it was painful along the way, I learned a lot and in the end, I am awfully glad it happened! In both cases it truly was for the best.

Maybe I will and maybe I won't become a published author, whether with this book or a different one in the future. Who knows? I am at peace with both of these things—as well as with *myself* now. Because I have gained life wisdom in this process that helps me cut through all sorts of my own bullshit barriers:

Life is too short to be miserable.

Handle your shit.

I don't have to live my life like everyone else.

Enjoy the path.

I may still be imperfect in applying these principles in my life, even though I do believe them deeply, but I'm getting there. And I am very much enjoying the path. Onward.

"Ageing is an extraordinary process where you become the person you always should have been." —David Bowie, English musician

Epilogue

"You never draw out of the deep of yourself that which you want; you always draw that which you are."

—Neville Goddard, Barbadian-American author

As I write this, it is now over a year since I left full-time employment in healthcare. Wow. What a ride. On this momentous occasion from this new perspective, I find myself questioning: was this a dumb idea? Am I just a big, lazy loser? Am I a failure? Have I fucked up my future? What does success even *mean*?

I didn't realize at the outset of this journey exactly how much I needed to step away from my healthcare career. I needed perspective and I needed clarity, but, above all, I really needed some goddamned rest! My heart was tired, my spirit in shambles, and my outlook on the rest of my working life stretching out ahead of me was grim at best.

I am now rested, at peace, and no longer engaged in a constant struggle with life. Man, things look a lot different now.

I have joy on a daily basis because I have made time for the things that give my life the most meaning: my husband and kids, dinking around with kitchen improv arts, helping my mom, hanging out with friends, growing plants. Traveling is more of a joy now that I don't have to ask for permission or worry about my personal time-off balance. I revel in cozy days spent reading good books, contemplating life, cuddling my dog, and writing to my heart's content. I love being in charge of how I use my time. If I want to go for a spontaneous walk in the middle of the afternoon because it is a beautiful fall day, I do that. And I enjoy the hell out of it! If my kid is home sick from school or my mom needs a trip to the ER, I can be there for them without also carrying the guilt and stigma of missing work. If my husband and I want to sneak off for a matinee, with wine and popcorn while everyone else is "at work", we do that. I no longer miss, or take for granted, the opportunities to really live.

I still work very part-time in healthcare and, surprisingly, I'm enjoying it again. Much more than I used to. But a year ago, or even three months ago, I was not sufficiently healed to find any fulfillment in this work at all. I was beyond empty and needed rest and time away to reset myself. It still sucks to hear people's tales of woe and the indifferent care they receive from the healthcare system, but the difference is that I no longer feel completely discouraged and drained by those stories. They are right; their experience as patients (myself included) is not what it should be. And probably won't be better anytime soon. This likely explains why my patients these days seem to like my visits so much—I have the time to listen and meet them wherever they are. I don't have an agenda to increase billable services, meet impossible visit quotas, get them to comply with evidence-based but generic recommendations or anything else that takes the "care" out of healthcare. I'm there to learn about them, evaluate their current health situation, and act as a resource. In my current role, I am actually—finally—providing the care that I believe people truly want and need. I listen to their troubles, complaints, aches and pains, and we discuss what health really means—for them. Then I provide feedback, encouragement, education and recommendations to help them get there. Together, we approach health as a complex construct that applies to everyone differently. What it means to be healthy is not (and never was) found in a generalized playbook designed by an insurance company. I'm not exaggerating or bragging when I say that sometimes people are almost moved to tears during visits with me. That's the power of real care right there and shows how hungry people are for it. Being in a position to serve patients in a way that I believe in, utilizing my education and years of experience, makes this work feel fulfilling again.

Does this mean I am going to chuck the writing dreams and go back to my healthcare career? Hell no! Healthcare is what I did, and sometimes still do. Writing is who I *am*. But at least I can experience the joy of helping others again in a part-time role that doesn't drain the lifeblood out of me anymore. And it helps finance my budding writing career that, as of yet, has paid me exactly zero dollars. But I finished the book that is in your hands and presumably you paid for it, so that bodes well. I think I've established for myself that amazing things can come from hope—and from leaping from the familiar and into the unknown. It sure beats complacency, anyhow.

And that brings me to the topic of security. I'm sure it's apparent to anyone who's read this far (for which I'm wildly grateful) that I still struggle with wanting security, especially financially. I don't have it all figured out yet, but somewhere deep inside of me is a desire to feel safe and protected, and money has somehow become inextricably tied to that. Feeling like loads of money in the bank or even just a steady paycheck is required for me to feel safe.

But would it? Keep me safe, that is. The intellectual answer is, obviously, no. Shit can always happen to get in the way. The stock market can crash, charlatans can steal all your money, you can be laid off, or have some unforeseen tragedy drain the bank balance (such as needing healthcare in the U.S.). So why do I persist in seeing financial security as anything other than a false idol, one that has a sneaky tendency to keep me apart from my dreams? Security does not equal success. In fact, it often hampers it. Security prevents growth and change by its very definition. I know this, and yet, I still want it at some basic, primal level.

Of course, this calls into question: do I really believe in myself and my resilience? Or does a lack of faith in myself keep me tied to looking for safety in the arms of financial stability? Maybe. But if I've learned anything in this past year, it's that time works wonders. It heals old wounds, aids perspective, and wears down the sharper edges of my own internal resistance to growth. It also helps new ideas take root, like this one: financial security has a place, but it is not the only—or even the most vital—element of success. I realize healthcare is never going to be my forever home, but at least I have peace now with spending time there to keep the ship afloat financially while I pursue more interesting endeavors. I am ok with this being enough for now and I am enjoying where I am at.

Falling out of love with my career has been the opposite of a predictable or comfortable experience, but I have grown a ton as an individual. And I am no longer miserable on a daily basis, trapped working in a broken system. Even if my book sales go nowhere and I just continue to earn a subsistence living from healthcare while writing my heart out, I am at a far better place than when I started. That's the beauty of "point C", as my husband would say. Sometimes the endpoint you think you want isn't actually where you *need* to go, so keep an open mind for where your road is leading you. For me, the journey has been beyond worthwhile even if I didn't go neatly and directly from A to B. Who wants boring or predictable, anyhow?

When I take an even longer look back—over the 10 years since my dad and brother died and shook me awake—I realize I have completely transformed my entire life. I mean, look at all that happened: I divorced, moved to a better state (sorry California) and learned to be a single mom. I took time to heal from my divorce, re-entered the dating world and joyfully remarried. Then I successfully left a poorly fitting career, made friends with my emotions, processed a lot of deep pain and wrote a book about it! I went from an unhappily married suburban mom and noble healthcare worker living a carefully created, but ultimately unfulfilling life to a person who takes big risks in pursuit of big dreams. I am no longer controlled by my fears as I pursue my own, unique way forward. That's *a lot* to be proud of!

I will close this book with the biggest compliment I have ever received (to date). To some it may not seem like a big deal, but to me, hearing these words had me overflowing with pride—

> "Oh KC, you have lived such an *interesting* life."

> —Sydney Rosener, dear friend and encourager

And you know what? She is right.

More Quotes

Quotes, to me, are islands of comfort in times of distress. I see them as little nuggets of wisdom from people smarter than me who've gone through similar shit. And survived. And learned from it. That's resilience. Take a shit-ton of lemons and don't just make lemonade, but also write the recipe for it so that others can benefit from your experience. In the year leading up to my 50th birthday, I collected 365 quotes, one for each day. I figured at that point in life I could use all the wisdom I could find. Maybe that collection will become a book one day as well. For now, here are just a few more I collected and found helpful during my career emigration.

Acceptance

"The first step toward change is awareness. The second is acceptance." —Nathaniel Branden

"I'm firmly convinced that true beauty only springs from the acceptance of oneself, from an awareness of who we really are." —Peter Lindbergh

"I slowly moved into an intellectual acceptance of what my intuition had always known." —Madeleine L'Engle

Anxiety

"If I take death into my life, acknowledge it, and face it square-ly, I will free myself from the anxiety of death and the pettiness of life—and only then will I be free to become myself." —Martin Heidegger

"Anxiety is the dizziness of freedom." —Søren Kierkegaard

"Anxiety is the handmaiden of creativity." —T.S. Eliot

"For as long as I can remember I have suffered from a deep feeling of anxiety which I have tried to express in my art." —Edvard Munch

"For me, most of the anxiety and difficulty of writing takes place in the act of not writing. It's the procrastination, the thinking about writing that is difficult." —Adam Mansbach

Commitment

"The difference between involvement and commitment is like ham and eggs. The chicken is involved, the pig is committed." —Martina Navratilova

"Unless commitment is made, there are only promises and hopes...but no plans." —Peter Drucker

"Courage, sacrifice, determination, commitment, toughness, heart, talent, guts. That's what little girls are made of." —Bethany Hamilton

Contentment

"Health is the greatest gift, contentment the greatest wealth, faithfulness the best relationship." —Buddha

"Contentment is the greatest treasure." —Lao Tzu

"When you are discontent, you always want more, more, more. Your desire can never be satisfied. But when you practice contentment, you can say to yourself, 'Oh yes, I already have everything that I really need.'" —Dalai Lama

Courage

"If you are lucky enough to find a way of life you love, you have to find the courage to live it." —John Irving

"Man cannot discover oceans unless he has the courage to lose sight of the shore." —André Gide

"Courage is being scared to death...and saddling up anyway." —John Wayne

Denial

"Denial ain't just a river in Egypt." —Mark Twain

Despair

"He who learns must suffer. And even in our sleep pain that cannot forget falls drop by drop upon the heart, and in our own despair, against our will, comes wisdom to us by the awful grace of God." —Aeschylus

"Transformation is a process, and as life happens there are tons of ups and down. It's a journey of discovery—there are moments on mountaintops and moments in deep valleys of despair." —Rick Warren

"Life begins on the other side of despair." —Jean-Paul Sartre

"Black and white are the colors of photography. To me they symbolize the alternatives of hope and despair to which mankind is forever subjected." —Robert Frank

Desperation

"The mass of men lead lives of quiet desperation. What is called resignation is confirmed desperation." —Henry David Thoreau

"Desperation is like stealing from the mafia; you stand a good chance of attracting the wrong attention." —Douglas Horton

"Lottery tickets are a surtax on desperation." —Douglas Coupland

"There's nothing like desperation to sharpen your sense of focus." —Thomas Newman

Disappointment

"We must accept finite disappointment, but never lose infinite hope." —Martin Luther King Jr.

"Disappointment builds character and strength." —Nafessa Williams

Disillusionment

"Just as an idealist metamorphoses into a crank right before turning into a full-fledged crackpot, I was bound to be disillusioned when the real world did not match my winged thoughts." —Kilroy J. Oldster

Discouragement

"Develop success from failures. Discouragement and failure are two of the surest stepping stones to success." —Dale Carnegie

"In spite of everything I shall rise again: I will take up my pencil, which I have forsaken in my great discouragement, and I will go on with my drawing." —Vincent Van Gogh

"Every great work, every big accomplishment, has been brought into manifestation through holding to the vision, and often just before the big achievement, comes apparent failure and discouragement." —Florence Scovel Shinn

Dissonance

"Dissonance is the truth about harmony." –Theodor W. Adorno

"Wisdom is tolerance of cognitive dissonance." —Robert Thurman

Doubt

"The fundamental cause of the trouble is that in the modern world the stupid are cocksure while the intelligent are full of doubt." —Bertrand Russell

Everyone has those days when you doubt yourself, and when you feel like everything you do sucks, but then there's those days when you feel like Superman. It's just the balance of the world. I just write to feel better." —Mac Miller

"Doubt is not a pleasant condition, but certainty is absurd." —Voltaire

Dread

"When the mind once allows a doubt to gain entrance, the value of deeds performed grow less, their character changes, we forget the past and dread the future." —Jules Verne

"The dread of evil is a much more forcible principle of human actions than the prospect of good." —John Locke

"What a folly to dread the thought of throwing away life at once, and yet have no regard to throwing it away by parcels and piecemeal." —John Howe

Dream

"If you can dream it, you can do it." —Walt Disney

"All men dream, but not equally. Those who dream by night in the dusty recesses of their minds, wake in the day to find that it was vanity: but the dreamers of the day are dangerous men, for they may act on their dreams with open eyes, to make them possible." —T. E. Lawrence

"To accomplish great things we must not only act, but also dream; not only plan, but also believe." —Anatole France

Ease

"True ease in writing comes from art, not chance, as those move easiest who have learnd [sic] to dance." —Alexander Pope

"Try to be like the turtle, at ease in your own shell." —Bill Copeland

"Being at ease with not knowing is crucial for answers to come to you." —Eckhart Tolle

Epiphany

"An artist's duty is rather to stay open-minded and in a state where he can receive information and inspiration. You always have to be ready for that little artistic epiphany." —Nick Cave

"Have you ever had that moment when you looked back on something and said, 'well, gosh, that seems obvious now...why didn't I see it then?' I like to call this Face Palm Epiphany. Oh, hindsight, you magical, humbling thing." —Alethea Kontis

"My junior year, I went to an LSAT-prep course. I flipped over my test and thought, 'You bastards.' I walked out and went to Waffle House. That's where I had what I call 'The Waffle House Epiphany': I didn't want to be a lawyer. I wanted to make a dent in the universe." —Alexis Ohanian

Excitement

"Learning should be a joy and full of excitement. It is life's greatest adventure; it is an illustrated excursion into the minds of the noble and the learned." —Taylor Caldwell

"It is always with excitement that I wake up in the morning wondering what my intuition will toss up to me, like gifts from the sea." —Jonas Salk

"I do not want to repeat myself. I want to reach for something I've never attained. This is the excitement of art." —T.C. Boyle

Faith

"Seeds of faith are always within us; sometimes it takes a crisis to nourish and encourage their growth." —Susan L. Taylor

"Faith is not belief without proof, but trust without reservation." —D. Elton Trueblood

"If fear is cultivated it will become stronger, if faith is cultivated it will achieve mastery." —John Paul Jones

"To have faith is to trust yourself to the water. When you swim you don't grab hold of the water, because if you do you will sink and drown. Instead you relax and float." —Alan Watts

"Leap and the net will appear." —Unknown

Fear

"The oldest and strongest emotion of man is fear, and the oldest and strongest kind of fear is fear of the unknown." —H.P. Lovecraft

"We can easily forgive a child who is afraid of the dark; the real tragedy of life is when men are afraid of the light." —Plato

"Do what you fear and fear disappears." —David Joseph Schwartz

"Only when we are no longer afraid do we begin to live." —Dorothy Thompson

"Fear is the beginning of wisdom." —William Tecumseh Sherman

"Humble souls are fearful of their own strength." —William Burnell

"Inaction breeds doubt and fear. Action breeds confidence and courage. If you want to conquer fear, do not sit home and think about it. Go out and get busy." —Dale Carnegie

Focus

"I don't focus on what I am up against. I focus on my goals and I try to ignore the rest." —Venus Williams

"Concentrate all your thoughts upon the work at hand. The sun's rays do not burn until brought to a focus." —Alexander Graham Bell

Freedom

"It is difficult to free fools from the chains they revere."
—Voltaire

"Freedom is the oxygen of the soul." —Moshe Dayan

"The only freedom which deserves the name is that of pursuing our own good, in our own way, so long as we do not attempt to deprive others of theirs or impede their efforts to obtain it."
—John Stuart Mill

"Freedom is from within." —Frank Lloyd Wright

Funk

"A lot of people can kick a ball a long way, but sometimes you get in a little funk and you work your way out of it." —Adam Vinatieri

Grief and Loss

"Death is not the greatest loss in life. The greatest loss is what dies inside us while we live." —Norman Cousins

"The most beautiful people we have known are those who have known defeat, known suffering, known struggle, known loss and have found their way out of those depths." —Elisabeth Kübler-Ross

"Grief is in two parts. The first is loss. The second is the remaking of life." —Anne Roiphe

Guilt

"Guilt is cancer. Guilt will confine you, torture you, destroy you as an artist. It's a black wall. A thief." —Dave Grohl

"Guilt: the gift that keeps on giving." —Erma Bombeck

"No work or love will flourish out of guilt, fear, or hollowness of heart, just as no valid plans for the future can be made by those who have no capacity for living now." —Alan Watts

Habit

"Good habits are hard to develop, but easy to live with; Bad habits are easy to develop but hard to live with. The habits that you have and the habits that have you will determine almost everything you achieve or fail to achieve." —Brian Tracy

Hope

"We must accept finite disappointment, but never lose infinite hope." —Martin Luther King Jr.

"Let your hopes, not your hurts, shape your future." —Robert H. Schuller

"To live without hope is to cease to live." —Fyodor Dostoevsky

Identity

"An identity would seem to be arrived at by the way in which the person faces and uses his experience." —James Baldwin

"In the social jungle of human existence, there is no feeling of being alive without a sense of identity." —Erik Erikson

"The ego is only an illusion, but a very influential one. Letting the ego-illusion become your identity can prevent you from becoming your true self." —Wayne Dyer

Imagination

"The world of reality has its limits; the world of imagination is boundless." —Jean-Jacques Rousseau

"Imagination is the eye of the soul." —Joseph Joubert

"To invent, you need a good imagination and a pile of junk." —Thomas A. Edison

"Logic will get you from A to B. Imagination will take you everywhere." —Albert Einstein

"The man who has no imagination has no wings." —Muhammad Ali

Impatience

"One of my weaknesses is impatience. I just have this aching need to get great things done. Can't stand slow change." —Robin Sharma

"Perhaps there is only one cardinal sin: impatience. Because of impatience we were driven out of paradise, because of impatience we cannot return." —W.H. Auden

Integrity

"The greatness of a man is not in how much wealth he acquires, but in his integrity and his ability to affect those around him positively." —Bob Marley

"The foundation stones for a balanced success are honesty, character, integrity, faith, love and loyalty." —Zig Ziglar

"Live so that when your children think of fairness, caring, and integrity, they think of you." —H. Jackson Brown Jr.

"If you have integrity, nothing else matters. If you don't have integrity, nothing else matters." —Alan K. Simpson

Melancholy

"I can barely conceive of a type of beauty in which there is no melancholy." —Charles Baudelaire

"Depression is melancholy minus its charms—the animation, the fits." —Susan Sontag

"All changes, even the most longed for, have their melancholy; for what we leave behind is a part of ourselves; we must die to one life before we can enter into another." —Gail Sheehy

Non-Conformity

"The opposite of courage is not cowardice, it is conformity. Even a dead fish can go with the flow." —Jim Hightower

"Conformity is the jailer of freedom and the enemy of growth." —John F. Kennedy

"If I ever found a place where I belonged, that in itself would be an identity crisis for me." —Mitski

"Your time is limited, so don't waste it living someone else's life." —Steve Jobs

Overwhelmed

"Sometimes when you are overwhelmed by a situation—when you're in the darkest of darkness—that's when your priorities are reordered." —Phoebe Snow

Peace

"You cannot find peace by avoiding life." —Virginial Woolf

"Peace cannot be kept by force; it can only be achieved by understanding." —Albert Einstein

"Those who are at war with others are not at peace with themselves." —William Hazlitt

"Peace comes from within, do not seek it without." —Buddha

"If there is to be any peace it will come through being, not having." —Henry Miller

"He that would live in peace and at ease must not speak all he knows or all he sees." —Benjamin Franklin

"The pursuit, even of the best things, ought to be calm and tranquil." —Marcus Tullius Cicero

"If everyone demanded peace instead of another television set, then there'd be peace." —John Lennon

Persistence

"Ambition is the path to success. Persistence in the vehicle you arrive in." —Bill Bradley

"Permanence, perseverance and persistence in spite of all obstacles, discouragements and impossibilities: It is this, that in all things distinguishes the strong soul form the weak." —Thomas Carlyle

Pride

"There are two kinds of pride, both good and bad. 'Good pride' represents our dignity and self-respect. 'Bad pride' is the deadly sin of superiority that reeks of conceit and arrogance." —John C. Maxwell

"I take a lot of pride in being myself. I'm comfortable with who I am." —James McAvoy

Regret

"It is better to look ahead and prepare, than to look back and regret." —Jackie Joyner-Kersee

"We crucify ourselves between two thieves: regret for yesterday and fear of tomorrow." —Fulton Oursler

"If you regret a mistake, don't just make that mistake again. Look at it and learn form it and grow from it." —Vitor Belfort

"I see it all perfectly; there are two possible situations—one can either do this or that. My honest opinion and my friendly advice is this: do it or do not do it—you will regret both." —Søren Kierkegaard

Resentment

"Our fatigue is often caused not by work, but by worry, frustration and resentment." —Dale Carnegie

"Resentment seems to have been given us by nature for a defense, and for a defense only! It is the safeguard of justice and the security of innocence." —Adam Smith

"I have a theory that burnout is about resentment. And you beat it by knowing what it is you're giving up that makes you resentful." —Marissa Meyer

Resilience

"Of course fear does not automatically lead to courage. Injury does not necessarily lead to insight. Hardship will not automatically make us better. Pain can break us or make us stronger. Suffering can destroy us or make us stronger. Fear can cripple us, or it can make us more courageous. It is resilience that makes the difference." —Eric Greitens

"In order to succeed, people need a sense of self-efficacy, to struggle together with resilience to meet the inevitable obstacles and inequalities of life." —Albert Bandura

"Persistence and resilience only come from having been given the chance to work through difficult problems." —Gever Tulley

"Indeed, this life is a test. It is a test of many things—of our convictions and priorities, our faith and our faithfulness, our patience and our resilience, and in the end, our ultimate desires." —Sheri L. Dew

"There will always be obstacles and challenges that stand in your way. Building mental strength will help you develop resilience to those potential hazards so you can continue on your journey to success." —Amy Morin

Resolve

"Wise to resolve and patient to perform." —Homer

"There is no scarcity of opportunity to make a living at what you love; there's only scarcity of resolve to make it happen." —Wayne Dyer

"Your success and happiness lies within you. Resolve to keep happy, and your joy and you shall form an invisible host against difficulties." — Helen Keller

"True courage is not the brutal force of vulgar heroes, but the firm resolve of virtue and reason." —Alfred North Whitehead

Risk

"If everything seems under control, then you're just not going fast enough." —Mario Andretti

"All courses of action are risky, so prudence is not in avoiding danger [it is impossible], but calculating risk and acting decisively. Make mistakes of ambition and not mistakes of sloth. Develop the strength to do bold things, not the strength to suffer." —Machiavelli (from *The Little Prince*)

Satisfaction

"Satisfaction of one's curiosity is one of the greatest sources of happiness in life." —Linus Pauling

"There are some days when I think I'm going to die from an overdose of satisfaction." —Salvador Dali

Security

"Make a radical change in your lifestyle and begin to boldly do things which you may previously never have thought of doing, or been too hesitant to attempt. So many people live within unhappy circumstances and yet will not take the initiative to change their situation because they are conditioned to a life of security, conformity, and conservation, all of which may appear to give one peace of mind, but in reality nothing is more damaging to the adventurous spirit within a man than a secure future." —Jon Krakauer

Self-Compassion

"As I look back and connect the dots, all I want to do is go back and hug my scared young self, who took a lot of steps out of impulse not knowing what will happen. So many nights of disappointment, so many others of being disillusioned where I would have just gone ahead and quit it all—I still do not know what kept me hanging in there." —Arfi Lamba

Shame

"Shame is the most powerful, master emotion. It's the fear that we're not good enough." —Brené Brown

"There is always shame in the creation of an expressive work, whether it is a book or a clay pot. Every artist worries about how they will be seen by others through their work. When you create, you aspire to do justice to yourself, to remake yourself, and there is always the fear that you will expose the very thing you hoped to transform." —Rachel Cusk

"Toil is no source of shame; idleness is shame." —Hesiod

"It would be impossible to estimate how much time and energy we invest in trying to fix, change and deny our emotions—especially the ones that shake us at our very core, like hurt, jealousy, loneliness, shame, rage and grief." —Debbie Ford

Validation

"Everything we do in our growing up has been done before. But it needs recognition and validation each time for each one of us—public, private, and secret." —Robert Fulghum

Eternal Thanks

I would not be who I am today or have written this book without the influence of these people in my life:

Nancy Jones: My third-grade teacher (and my first editor)

Max Mitchell: The only high school teacher who "got me" (also, he was cool, played the drums, and is probably part of the reason why I prefer hairy men. Rest in peace, Mr. Mitchell)

Gary Chamberlain: Seattle University professor of religion (who believed I had something unique and interesting to say)

Mary Ersek: RN, PhD Seattle University nursing professor (an early idol and mentor)

Rhea McCormack: Hospice bereavement counselor (who helped me grieve—and who also believed I was destined for greater things)

Brian Copperstein: hospice social worker (who held my hand in the early days of grief and gave me confidence that I was doing it right)

Sherellen Gerhart: Hospice MD (treasured friend and sounding board)

Mike Carpenter: Brother (best friend, and confidant; rest in peace, my brother)

Sydney Rosener: Worker bee colleague (treasured friend and unfailing encourager)

Judy Wooten: Best hospice manager I could hope for when going through shit times (treasured friend)

[Unnamed bad boss]: Provided a big push I needed to change my life

Christina Beck: Daughter from another mother (kindred spirit)

Darlene Pruessmann: Lifelong friend (who has always believed I have wisdom worth sharing)

Mom: Inspired my love of reading which led to my love of writing

Dad: Shared a love of talking about the deeper questions in life and believed deeply in enjoying the path (Rest in peace, Dad)

Not people, but: The University of California at Berkeley taught me philosophy (with a side of ingenuity, resilience and rebellion) and Seattle University honed my critical thinking skills and encouraged exploration and leaps of faith

Nora and Zack Nelson: Kids (eternal joys of my world who inspire me to set a good example for them)

Steven Shomler: Husband (this book is dedicated to him, even though words fall short of my feelings of gratitude)

Books

These books helped me become the me who wrote this book:

Gift From the Sea — Anne Morrow Lindbergh

My Life in France — Julia Child

Self-Compassion — Kristen Neff

Broken Open — Elizabeth Lesser

When Things Fall Apart — Pema Chödrön

Quiet: The Power of Introverts in a World That Can't Stop Talking — Susan Cain

Hunger and *Bad Feminist* — Roxane Gay

A Good Year — Peter Mayle

You Are a Badass and *You Are a Badass at Making Money* — Jen Sincero

Change Your Thoughts, Change Your Life — Wayne Dyer

Love and Work — Marcus Buckingham

The War of Art and *Turning Pro* — Steven Pressfield

Tribes and *The Dip* — Seth Godin

On Writing — Stephen King

Greenlights — Mathew McConaughey

Losing My Virginity — Sir Richard Branson

The Third Door — Alex Banayan

Kitchen Confidential — Anthony Bourdain

Mortality — Christopher Hitchens

The Year of Magical Thinking — Joan Didion

Playlist

The soundtrack for writing this book:

Sorrow and *Changes*— David Bowie

It's the End of the World —REM

Ball & Chain — Social Distortion

Free Fallin' — Tom Petty and the Heartbreakers

Watching the *Wheels* — John Lennon

Start Me Up and *Satisfaction* — Rolling Stones

It's Now or Never — Elvis Presley

The Edge of Glory – Lady Gaga

Band on the Run — Paul McCartney and Wings

Under Pressure — Queen and David Bowie

Low Budget— The Kinks

I wanna Be Sedated — Ramones

In My Life — The Beatles

All These Things That I've Done — The Killers

My Way — Frank Sinatra

You Really Got Me — both The Kinks and Van Halen versions

Brick House — Commodores

Lust For Life — Iggy Pop

Don't Stop Me Now – Queen

My Hero — Foo Fighters

Cry, Cry, Cry — Johnny Cash

What a Wonderful World — Louis Armstrong

There She Goes — The La's

At Last — Etta James

Snacks

These snacks sustained me while writing this book:

Cheez-Its

Pringles

Coke Zero

Whisps

Chili Cheese Fritos

Bell peppers (all colors)

Pirate's Booty

Pink Lady apples

Earl Grey tea

Flamin' Hot Cheetos (but hate the orange fingers)

Cherry sours

Ramen noodles (served dry, seasoning packet sprinkled on top)

End Credits

I believe books are like movies – a group effort. I may have written this book, but I had A LOT of help getting it to this final form and into your hands. That's why I am going to do my best to recognize all of the players here, just like they do in the movies:

Concept: KC Shomler

Book Development and Title: KC Shomler and Steven Shomler

Writer: KC Shomler

Inspiration: Nora and Zack Nelson

Author Nurture: Steven Shomler

Early Readers and Supporters of the Dream: Paul Barth, Christina Beck, Jenn David Connolly, Sherellen Gerhart, Darlene Pruessmann, Steven Shomler, Garry Taylor, Jennifer Young

Editor: Rob Peace

Assistant Editors: Christina Beck, Darlene Pruessmann, KC Shomler, Steven Shomler

Formatting: KC Shomler

Formatting Software: Atticus

Cover Design: Jenn David Connolly

Author Photograph: Steven Shomler

Publisher: Bonfire Books Press

Website Design, Creation and Support: Arthur Breur

Marketing and marketing strategy: Steven Shomler, Christina Beck

Staffing: Upwork

Indispensable remote writing support device: Apple Watch voice memo app

Tools: Pilot Precise V5 extra fine in blue and lined steno pads

Printing and distribution: Ingram Spark, KDP

Emotional Support: Nash Nelson

This book was written on a Lenovo Yoga laptop, circa 2020 utilizing Microsoft Word